The Critter CONTROL Handbook

Pro Secrets for Stopping Sneaky Squirrels & Other Crafty Critters in Their Tracks

Dan "The Critter Man" **Hershey**

D0608233

Voyageur Press

Edited by Kari A. Cornell
Designed by JoDee Turner
Printed in China

02 03 04 05 06 5 4 3 2 1

Library of Congress Cataloging-in-Publication Data
Hershey, Dan, 1953-
    The critter control handbook : pro secrets for stopping sneaky squir-rels & other crafty critters in their tracks / Dan Hershey.
        p. cm.
    ISBN 0-89658-588-3 (alk. paper)
        1. Ground Squirrels—Control. 2. Wildlife pests—Control. I. Title.

SB994.S67 H47 2001
632'.6—dc21

                                                    2001046792

Distributed in Canada by Raincoast Books, 9050 Shaughnessy Street, Vancouver, B.C. V6P 6E5

Published by Voyageur Press, Inc.
123 North Second Street, P.O. Box 338, Stillwater, MN 55082 U.S.A.
651-430-2210, fax 651-430-2211
books@voyageurpress.com
www.voyageurpress.com

The information in this book is carefully researched, accurate, and complete to the best of our knowledge. All recommendations are made without any guarantee on the part of the author or Voyageur Press. The author and publisher disclaim any liability in connection with the direct or indirect use of this information.

We recognize that some words, models names, and designations mentioned herein are the property of the trademark holder. We use them for identification purposes only. Where trade names are used, no discrimination is intended nor endorsement implied.

Educators, fundraisers, premium and gift buyers, publicists, and market-ing managers: Looking for creative products and new sales ideas? Voyageur Press books are available at special discounts when purchased in quanti-ties, and special editions can be created to your specifications. For details contact the marketing department at 800-888-9653.

Front cover photo by Bill Hollister

Acknowledgments

I would like to thank the New York State Department of Environmental Conservation Wildlife Pathology Unit for use of their excellent slides of wildlife diseases. I also thank George Froehlich, Paul Berry, Bill Hollister, Pam Berry, and my wife, Amy, for their helpful suggestions and photographic contributions.

Disclaimer

The purpose of this book is to provide a helpful set of guidelines to solving problems with wildlife. Methods and techniques described in this book have worked successfully for the author.

Keep in mind that every nuisance wildlife situation is different and that wild animals are unpredictable. The author has made every attempt to alert the reader to laws pertaining to nuisance wildlife. Before controlling any situation, the reader should check with local law enforcement officials to make sure the chosen method is legal.

The author cannot be held responsible for any actions taken as a result of reading this book. Anyone placing a trap, poison, repellent, deterrent, or using a firearm assumes the responsibility and consequences of their own actions.

Where trade names are used, no endorsement is intended, nor is criticism implied of similar products not named.

Contents

Preface

I have always been fascinated with wildlife and its relationship with people. While most guys growing up in my central Connecticut suburban city were into cars, sports, and girls, my mind was usually on finding a new muskrat house on our pond, chasing geese off the local golf course, or building a better mousetrap. (Well, okay, I did think about girls a lot, too, but that's another story!)

It was only natural that some of my early outdoor adventures led me to become the Nuisance Wildlife Control Officer (NWCO) I am today. Over the years I've learned that there is much more to wildlife management (critter control) than just setting a trap and catching an animal. One of the most important lessons I've learned is that the interactions between people and wild animals can and usually will vary greatly. How people exist and interact with wildlife depends in large part on the individuals involved. For example, some people love to hear the honk of golf course geese flying in to feed, while others, slipping in goose droppings on the way to the next putting green, learn to hate the birds. And everybody loves a beaver until it is in their backyard, chewing on their ornamental trees and flooding their septic system. For the most part, people enjoy watching wildlife from a distance. It's when a critter enters a family's living space and starts eating electrical wire insulation, urinating on ceiling tiles, or causing any number of other problems, that my phone begins to ring.

Watching and learning about wildlife is still my favorite pastime. You can't control critters if you don't understand them. Knowing what they eat, where they hide, where they like to live, and where they will and won't go, is all part of the fun of nuisance wildlife control.

In my twenty years of helping homeowners control nuisance wildlife, I have learned many tricks of the trade. In this book I offer proven techniques that really work! If there is one thing that I have learned in this business, it's that there are a lot of people out there ready to take your money for products and techniques that simply don't work! Beware of the person who tries to sell you an ultrasound device to scare away birds (they can't hear it) or poison peanuts to get rid of moles (they eat earthworms). My book is packed with useful facts about all kinds of animals so that you can educate yourself and not be taken advantage of. Did you know, for example, that sliced bananas are the best bait for woodchucks? Or that if you hang a mousetrap, you will catch twice as many mice than if you set it on the floor? Read on for many more invaluable tips.

Introduction

In New York State, Nuisance Wildlife Control Officers receive more than 11,000 calls each year.

"There's a squirrel in my attic!"

"There's a skunk in my window well!"

"How do I get this x#x#x# woodchuck out of my garden?"

But nuisance wildlife is not just a problem in the state of New

Whitetail deer populations are growing at alarming rates—and so are the complaints about them.

York—wild animals stir up trouble anywhere they're found. Nuisance wildlife has become more disruptive in recent decades. In the early 1900s, experts claim that there were as few as 500,000 deer in the United States. Whitetail numbers are now estimated at more than 15 million! There is no question that the numbers of deer, squirrel, and raccoon are exploding. And, as more people move from the cities to the suburbs, the potential for human/animal conflict increases.

As wildlife populations grow and their habitats disappear, animals are more and more likely to appear on private property. Animals can provide hours of entertainment. I love to watch the V formation of geese flying overhead or a handsome buck eating apples underneath my apple tree. These same animals that entertain one day may damage property and cause a homeowner considerable expense the next (i.e. goose droppings on the lawn or orchard damage from deer).

Wildlife can cause a variety of problems. Damage to property tops the list, including, but certainly not limited to, squirrels chewing through fascia and soffits, woodchucks and raccoons eating garden veggies, and skunks digging up lawns in search of grubs. The second most common complaint is of animal annoyance, such as bats flying around inside the home or woodpeckers tapping on the side of the house in search of insects. Reports of sick animals and of wildlife harassing domestic pets are third and fourth on the list. Complaints about some species of animals far outweigh complaints about others. In New York State, squirrels top the list for the most complaints on record. Raccoons are a close second, followed by skunks, woodchucks, bats, and opossums.

I've found that people have strong prejudices toward different species of wildlife. For example, most people request that raccoons be released unharmed. Many want deer and geese repelled, but not harmed. More often than not, clients want skunks destroyed and almost everyone wants rats and mice removed from the face of the earth! In this book, I take all attitudes into account. And yes, I even describe live-trapping techniques for rats and mice!

Attitudes toward nuisance wildlife have changed over the years. The generation of grandparents who would pick up a shotgun to blast the raccoon eating their sweet corn has given way to electric fences and "Havahart" live traps. Keep in mind that there is almost always a nonlethal alternative to wildlife control. I always recommend nonlethal methods first. Unfortunately, there are some circumstances where lethal control techniques are the only solutions guaranteed to solve your problem. For example, the fox or coyote that develops a taste for domestic cat will usually continue to kill our feline friends until it is stopped for good. Also, animals sick with rabies must be destroyed for testing purposes, especially when humans have been in contact with the diseased animal. This book is designed to provide the homeowner with the most current, effective, and humane control methods available.

Most people want raccoons captured and released without harm.

1

Identifying the Problem

Knowing the identity of the critter is the first step in solving any nuisance wildlife problem. Only after you know what you're up against can you hatch a plan for the animal's capture, relocation, removal, or, in the worst-case scenario, its extermination. Many times you may catch only a fleeting glimpse of the animal making it difficult to identify. Other times you may not see the animal at all, but see only the clues it left behind.

Most people can identify a tree chewed by a beaver or the network of runways dug by moles when searching for earthworms. But sometimes the clues aren't as obvious and the animal causing the problem is unknown. I often get calls from homeowners who know that they have a problem animal, but don't know what it is. It is usually a combination of factors that help me determine how to proceed. Clues to the mystery guest may be found in any of the following.

This chewed tree is a typical sign of beavers in the area.

Its Size

You might be surprised at how many people don't know the difference between a raccoon, a woodchuck, or a mink. Paying attention to the animal's size, shape, and color can help to identify the animal. Unfortunately, sometimes the homeowner only catches a quick glimpse of the critter as it runs from the garden to the woods or across the kitchen floor. More than once I have found myself asking questions like, Was it bigger than a football? Smaller than a tennis ball? Did it have a long or short tail? Was its body round or long and skinny? Did the tail have obvious hair or was it hairless?

It's easy to confuse a raccoon and a woodchuck, especially when you only get a quick look. Time of day will help determine if it is a coon or chuck. Woodchucks rarely venture out after dark and, unless raccoons are sick, they are seldom out during the daytime. Both animals are active in the twilight hours.

Its Color

Comparing color is often a good way to distinguish one animal from another. An opossum and a skunk are similar in size, but are usually very different in color. The skunk has a black

body with a white stripe on its back. An opossum is grayish white and has a rat-like, hairless tail. But some skunks can be almost all white, often looking very similar to the grayish white color of the opossum. If in doubt, check the tail: In contrast to the opossum's hairless tail, a skunk's tail is large and bushy.

Raccoons are grayish brown, like a variety of other animals, but their black and brown ringed tail and black face mask make raccoons unique. Most bats are brown, with black, webbed wings and ears. Woodchucks, muskrats, and beavers are reddish brown. Gray fox and coyotes are silvery gray with some brown highlights. Keep in mind, too, that coloring varies in most animals. For example, I have seen some reddish versions of the coyote, an animal that is usually gray.

The gray fox (top) and the eastern coyote (bottom) have similar coloring, but the fox tends to be smaller than the coyote. The eastern coyote also looks very much like its cousin, the wolf.

Droppings (Feces)

If the animal has left droppings on your property, you're in luck (so to speak). The color, shape, quantity, and content of animal droppings or feces can tell you lot about the animal. The size of the pellet is not always indicative of the animal's size. Deer for example, leave many small, marble-shaped dark brown droppings in one spot. Rabbits leave similar round droppings, but they are lighter brown and fewer in number.

Bat droppings and mouse droppings can also be confused. Generally mouse droppings are straight while bat droppings have a slight curl to them. Mouse droppings usually contain small seeds and grains, while bat droppings consist of digested insects.

Fox and coyote droppings are usually cigar shaped, with animal bones and fur mixed throughout. The ends of fox or coyote droppings are usually pointed. For some reason these animals like to leave their mark in obvious places such as the middle of a trail, on top of flat rocks, or next to tree stumps. An adult coyote dropping will be slightly larger than an adult fox dropping. Fox droppings are usually about the width of a pinky finger while coyote droppings are about as wide as a thumb. It is most difficult to differentiate adult fox droppings from immature coyote droppings, as they are similar in size and content.

Raccoon and opossum feces are also cigar shaped, but are not usually pointed on the ends. Seeds, a big part of their diet, are especially obvious in their feces. These animals commonly defecate at the base of large trees and in the crotches of limbs on these large trees. Woodchucks have much smaller droppings than raccoons. Since woodchucks are mostly grass eaters, their feces are dark brown and have nothing identifiable within them.

Geese and male turkeys have similar droppings. They are both shaped like a letter *J*. Geese generally eat grass, so their droppings are green and fibrous, while gobbler droppings tend to be black and white, due to the insects and mast crops (such as acorns) that make up the bulk of their diet. Hen turkey droppings are shaped like a Hershey's Kiss. Anyone who spends a lot of time at a golf course or a cemetery (since geese tend to congregate in these places) should be able to describe goose droppings.

Its Nest or Den

The type of nest an animal builds and where it decides to build it can help identify the animal. Gray squirrels commonly build large leafy nests high up in mature trees. But when the squirrel population exceeds the number of trees available, the critters may find their way into chimneys, attics, or old abandoned buildings. Squirrels may still bring in leaves to make their nests, but I have seen them improvise with such items as insulation,

Deer droppings

Rabbit droppings

newspaper, and clothing. I have seen instances where squirrels have chewed through fascia, soffits, and sidewalls to make nest.

Most people are familiar with the dome-shaped lodge that a beaver builds. Muskrats make similar lodges, but instead of using chewed sticks, they use vegetation such as cattails. Keep in mind that the beaver and muskrat don't always make a lodge. If the bank is high enough along a pond or stream, they may burrow into the bank, leaving no visible sign above the water's edge. Under the water you may see runways leading to the den. In both situations there is usually a nest of vegetation inside the den where the mother will give birth to her young. You can tell if these dens are active by looking at the water's edge. If there is a lot of activity, the water will have a murky line extending out from the shore. If you can see a runway, feel the bottom of it to see if it is hard and compacted or soft and silty. If it is hard, you can be certain somebody is home. If there is vegetation and silt, the run hasn't been used for a while. In the winter, if there is clear ice on the pond and the hole is active, a line of bubbles leaving the bank and extending out into the pond for several feet will reveal the animal's whereabouts.

These baby raccoons were born in the soffit of a neighbor's garage.

Geese and ducks normally make their nests on the ground fairly close to the water's edge. Wood ducks are an exception. They have their young in a hollow tree or in a manmade wood-duck box. Most of the time, waterfowl prefer to nest on an island out in the middle of a pond where they are less vulnerable to raccoon attacks. Occasionally, predators put so much pressure on nesting waterfowl that the birds will travel long distances away from the water to hatch their eggs. This year a mallard hen decided to nest in the ornamental bushes along the main entrance to my very active six-story office building located near Albany, New York. The nearest pond was more than a mile (1.6 km) away.

Holes in the ground may lead to the home of a variety of animals. Moles, voles, rabbits, skunks, chipmunks, mice, rats, fox, opossums, snakes, bees, and woodchucks all tunnel holes in the ground in which to have their young. The size of a hole provides clues to its resident. Yellow jackets and ground bees make a hole the width of a pencil. Snakes, mice, voles, and moles make a hole the size of a quarter. Rats and chipmunks make a hole the size of a one-half dollar. Rabbits, skunks, opossums, and woodchucks all have entry holes about the size of a softball. Rabbits, skunks, and opossums do not dig holes themselves. They usually occupy abandoned woodchuck holes. Even a fox will use a woodchuck den, widening the hole a little to make it just right.

Raccoons often make their nests in a hollow tree, in the eaves of old buildings or barns, in unused chimneys, and sometimes in an abandoned woodchuck den. Most nests are lined with hay or straw.

Opossums will make their nests in trees, in the ground, or in old buildings. One unfortunate client of mine had a mother opossum raising young in her underwear drawer! The mother opossum found a way into the mobile home via a bathroom vent pipe. It climbed into the backside of her dresser and built its nest.

Mice love to make their nests in stone walls, building walls, insulation, and just about any other place you can imagine, provided it is somewhat private. I have found mice nests in my ice skates, in my Coleman camp stove, in the map pocket on the driver's side door of my minivan, and inside the muffler of my lawnmower. Mice nests are usually made of fur, vegetation, twine, clothing, and paper materials. They are ball-like and loosely woven together.

Many bees and wasps make either a mud or paper nest. Paper nests can be found in trees and around the eaves of buildings. I have found smaller nests in metal tubing items such as clothesline poles, swing sets, and iron stair railings. Wild honeybees usually make their home in hollow trees, although I have seen one residence in which the bees had built a nest in the living room wall. The honey eventually soaked through the wall, leaving a very sticky mess. The wall had to be replaced.

One of the most interesting bees is the cicada killer. This very large bee digs a pencil-sized hole in the ground about 3 to 4 inches (7.6 to 10.2 cm) deep. The bee finds a grasshopper, paralyzes it, brings it to the bottom of the hole, and lays its eggs on it. When the young are born, they have a fresh food supply. They are most often found where the ground is sandy and quite dry.

Yellow jacket nests are underground and can often be quite large, depending on the number of bees. Most nests are about the size of a softball, but I have seen them much larger. When making their nest, yellow jackets excavate the hole by rolling little balls of clay, carrying them out, and dropping them anywhere from 6 to 20 feet (1.8 to 6.1 m) from the entrance. One client complained that something was dropping dirt balls on him and his car. Once I saw the little clay balls, I was able to find the nest and get rid of them.

This is an example of a buck rub, made by a buck deer rubbing its antlers against the bark.

Pigeons nest on roadway underpasses, bridges, and old brick buildings, including window ledges of homes and churches. Constructed of grass and sticks, pigeon nests house mites, lice, and other parasites. In flying to and from their nests, pigeons defecate, leaving unsightly marks on the sides of buildings.

On a recent trip to my family's camp in upstate Vermont, my father-in-law complained that he couldn't sleep in the upstairs loft because he was itching so much. I suspected fiberglass was the reason, since the roof had been insulated. I asked him to collect some dust from the upstairs. Microscopic identification revealed many dead bird mites in the dust. Armed with this information, he went back to the cabin and located two bird nests close to the window where he had been sleeping. One nest had several dead baby birds in it.

Rabbit chewings such as this can look very much like a buck rub.

Marks or Sign It Leaves

The trained eye can identify a nuisance animal from the marks or sign it leaves behind. Raccoons, for example, often leave smudge marks on the sides of buildings. Their muddy feet soil the siding where they routinely go up and down. A close look at any sharp edges of siding may also reveal gray hairs from the animal.

Raccoons and squirrels have very sharp claws that leave scratch marks on the trees and buildings they climb. Most trees and bird feeders are scarred with such scratch marks.

Small holes in wood siding are either the result of wood

boring bees or woodpeckers. I recently built a pine building and found that bumblebees love to bore into the freshly cut pine. Unlike woodpeckers, these bees left a small pile of fine sawdust behind as evidence. Woodpeckers leave many holes and fairly large chunks of wood behind.

Evidence of a deer in the area may be visible on the trunk of a tree. A few years back, a man from a local nursery showed me a piece of maple sapling that he thought had been girdled by some type of animal. The tree had died and he wanted to know what had killed it. One look at the sapling and I recognized the rub as one made by a buck deer. I explained to him that male deer rub their antlers on saplings in the fall of the year. Bucks can be very aggressive to trees, sometimes breaking branches right off.

Sometimes when an animal chews on a tree, the marks can look a lot like deer rubs. Rabbits often girdle saplings, particularly sumac, which can look very much like a deer rub. One way to tell the difference between the two is to check their distance from the ground. Deer rubs are usually 3 or 4 feet (.9 or 1.2 m) above the ground, while rabbit chewings are at ground level. About 2 feet (.6 m) of snow, however, can raise the height of the rabbit chewings to the same level as a deer rub.

The clean break on these twigs is a sure sign that a rabbit, with its razor-sharp teeth, did the damage.

It's easy to mistake rabbit chewings with deer chewings, too. One way to differentiate between the two is to look at the end of the chewed bushes. Deer have to grind off a twig, leaving the end looking ragged. Rabbits have very sharp teeth and are able to cleanly cut off the twig.

Skunks leave two types of marks while searching for grubs in the lawn. Many small holes in the brown areas of the lawn are the most common sign of skunks. Skunks use

The jagged breaks to these twigs indicate deer damage.

their sense of smell and hearing to track down the grubs. Then they use their paws to dig holes ½ inch (1.3 cm) wide and 3 inches (7.6 cm) deep to catch the grubs. Every now and then a rogue skunk decides to really rip up a lawn in search of grubs. When this happens, the skunk reaches under the sod and flips it over, looking for the grub. Brown patches in the grass are usually the only places dug up. The grass is brown because grubs killed the roots of the grass.

If the nuisance animal has been digging in your trash, the animal's method for ripping into a plastic garbage bag may reveal its identity. Raccoons will rip a garbage bag to shreds or certainly tear it up to get at what's inside. Opossums will also tear things up but not as much as coons. Skunks will rip only a very small hole at the exact spot they want to reach. Rats will also leave very small holes in the bag.

How It Attacks or Kills Other Animals

Sometimes the way an animal kills or leaves marks on another animal will tell you about the killer. Most complaints of this nature pertain to chicken coop marauders. Mink, weasels, rats,

A skunk, in search of grubs, made these holes in the lawn.

This is a grub, similar to the one the skunk was after.

fox, opossums, raccoons, and hawks will all attack the domestic chicken or its eggs. Hawks attack from the air and can be deterred by covering the coop with netting or chicken wire. Hawks, weasels, and mink go for the birds' heads, first; hawks rip off the head. Weasels and mink bite the back of the head, leaving a tiny bite mark. Raccoons and fox kill the chicken at the site then quickly drag it away. Opossums maul and eat the animal at the site.

If you are missing eggs in the chicken coop or you find little pieces of shell, I would put my money on raccoons. If most of the shell is there but it has a small hole in it, I would bet on rats.

Not too long ago I had a homeowner complain to me that some kind of an animal had killed one of her two cats and had injured the other one. The injured cat had obvious puncture marks on its rump and hind legs. She had seen a gray fox in the area, but didn't think a fox would be capable of attacking her large cat. I explained to her that the puncture marks were definitely from some type of canine, possibly a domestic dog, a fox, or a coyote. Canines usually go for the rump and crotch of an animal first. I was suspicious of the fox. I told her to keep an eye on the cat for a few days. She called me the next day to tell me that she saw the fox chase the cat into her barn. That evening, per her instructions, I came back with a flashlight, a shotgun, and a predator call. (The predator call I used was similar to a duck call. It has a thin reed on the end that you blow into and plastic bellows on the other end to make the sound of an injured rabbit. The predator, thinking that an easy meal lies just over the ridge, comes running to investigate.) It has been my experience that once a fox or coyote has tasted domestic cat, it will continue to hunt them. The only option in this case is to kill the predator. After a few rabbit squeals on the call, and one shotgun blast, the fox never bothered another cat again.

The Sounds It Makes

Mice and squirrels can make an awful lot of noise when they are in your walls. I have received many complaints about squirrels in walls, only to find that the noise was really from mice. Mice can, and do, make as much noise as squirrels. Most of the sounds you will hear are from them scampering, scratching, and chewing inside the walls or ceiling. There are a couple of ways to determine whether you have mice or squirrels. Mice are not very vocal, but squirrels are. Squirrels tend to make a growling noise while the most you'll hear from a mouse is an occasional squeak. Making note of the time of day that you hear the noise may also help determine what is inside your walls. Mice will be active whenever the room is quiet, usually all through the night. Squirrels will not be in the house during most of the daylight hours, except when the mother has young, but will be active at daybreak and at dusk.

In the spring and summer months I often get complaints about coyotes howling and scaring people. Not only do coyotes howl (especially during spring mating season), they yip and bark, much like a German shepherd barks at the mailman. I have one family of coyotes that I can locate any night I want, just by waiting for the horns and noise of the 8:20 P.M. Amtrak train. As soon as the train is close by, they start yipping and howling. Fire sirens, police sirens, and ambulance sirens trigger the same response.

Foxes don't howl like coyotes, but they do yip when chasing rabbits, much like a beagle will bark when giving chase.

Quick Tip

Listening is the best way to determine whether you have mice or squirrels. Mice are not very vocal, but squirrels are. Squirrels tend to make a growling noise while the most you'll hear from a mouse is an occasional squeak. And, mice are active all night long, while squirrels are most active at daybreak and at dusk.

On a clear summer night, it is very common to hear foxes chasing rabbits on my back hill. To the unknowing, it might sound very similar to a poodle at the back door, yipping to be let in.

Raccoons make a variety of noises, the most common one sounding much like a chortle. They will also squeal and screech, mostly when fighting. At times, raccoons become intoxicated from eating fermented grapes and sumac berries. Drunk raccoons make a lot of noise. Male deer grunt like pigs during the mating season. Female and young deer blat and bleat much like sheep. All deer will snort and blow to alert other deer of potential danger. Woodchucks let out a high-pitched whistle when danger is nearby, alerting all other woodchucks to be careful. Bats make a quiet clicking sound when flying, when disturbed, or while roosting.

Usually rabbits make almost no noise. But when a rabbit is under attack by a predator such as a hawk, fox, or coyote, it will make a noise that sounds like a baby crying. This sound is often duplicated by using a predator call to lure hungry predators such as fox and coyote into the range of a hunter's sight.

When alarmed, garter snakes emit a foul odor.

Its Odor

Talk of animals with odors almost always brings to mind the skunk. But the truth is, many animals give off odors. Both garter snakes and turtles can give off a very foul odor when startled or harassed. Mink and weasels release an unpleasant odor from glands similar to that of the skunk—and they are capable of spraying it much like their black-and-white relative. Muskrats and beavers have a musk or castor gland that releases a pleasant, sweet-smelling odor used to mark their territory or to attract a mate during the breeding season. The smell of mouse and squirrel urine can be extremely annoying, especially if the critters are living in your ceiling or walls. For information on combating specific animal odors, see chapter 8.

What It Eats

A study of what and how a nuisance animal is eating can also help you identify the animal. If the animal eats meat, for example, it's more than likely a canine. If the nuisance animal is a vegetarian, you're probably dealing with a muskrat or a beaver. Is the animal raiding fruit or crops? Then it's probably a raccoon.

There are some exceptions to these rules, however. Fox will eat rabbits and mice, but they also love fruit, especially grapes. Raccoon like fish, sweet corn, grapes, and acorns. Squirrels eat acorns, seeds, and, unfortunately, everything that I put in my bird feeder. Bats eat mostly insects, consuming more than 1,000 mosquitoes in an hour. Snapping turtles, otters, and great blue herons eat mostly fish. Snakes eat insects and mice. Ducks and geese eat grass and vegetation.

Cattail roots floating along the edge of a pond or stream is sure indication that there is a muskrat nearby. Cattail roots are quite white and muskrats usually bite them into 1-inch-long (2.5-cm) chunks. If the bark on a tree has been chewed, it could be a beaver, a porcupine, a rabbit, or maybe even a deer. Beaver damage is easy to spot from the large chunks of wood lying beneath the stump. The type of tree that is damaged provides clues, too. Rabbits love sumac bark. Deer like sumac, too, but they usually just nibble on the buds. Porcupine girdle large areas of hemlock bark, usually higher up in the trees.

How It Eats

How an animal eats can help the trained eye figure out who the culprit is. For example, deer tend to grind up plants before biting them off while rabbits slice plant tips off with their razor-sharp teeth. Sweet corn damage can be caused by a variety of animals ranging from deer, to raccoons, to squirrels, to wild turkeys. A close look at the damage can tell you a lot. Raccoons will climb up the stalk and bend it over to the ground. They concentrate on a specific area of the field and work through the night to eat the corn at the site. Large areas of bent over corn stalks are usually along the edges of the field and areas closest to the woods, where raccoons can retreat for safety if necessary.

Squirrels will also climb a cornstalk, but do not bend it over or break it off. Squirrels are daytime feeders. They chew off the ear of corn and carry it into the woods. Squirrels will

Deer like to root through cut cornfields in search of leftover ears.

Try sprinkling flour in the animal's high-traffic area to see prints when tracks aren't visible on the ground.

Muskrat tracks. Note the tail drag marks in the snow.

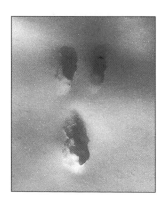

Rabbit tracks

leave the ears of corn in tree crotches; they also leave cleaned-off cobs along trails leading to and from the field.

Deer feed in the evening, just before dark. Even before the corn is half grown, deer start eating the plant. They work the edges of the field, chewing the fresh green tops of the plant. Once the corn produces ears, they will try to eat what is on the stalk, starting at the silk end, often bending it to the ground. They may try to break it off and eat it on the ground. Deer don't concentrate on one spot like the raccoon does. Instead they work the edges of the field, meandering through the rows, searching for an ear that is easy to chew. I have one farmer friend who claims that wild turkeys do a lot of damage to his corn. When the ears reach the height of the turkeys' heads, the birds peck the ear until it is all gone. He has a flock of about fifty turkeys that can rapidly eat a lot of corn. I am always welcome there during turkey-hunting season.

The Tracks It Makes

Many books have been written on animal tracks and I will not attempt to duplicate them here. What I can give you is a crash course on the track marks of some of the more common nuisance animals and I can also provide some photographs to help you with identification.

When tracks are nowhere to be seen and I want to find out who the mystery guest is, I sprinkle a fine layer of flour in front of the animal's hole or on the trail the animal appears to be using. If there is fine sand, sometimes I just smooth it off and come back in a day or so. This is a great way to find out if the animal is still active in the area and it gives you some really nice prints. Another way to find out if the animal's home is still in use is to prop some small sticks across the hole. Check back the next day to see if the animal has moved the sticks aside.

If you have some good prints to study, ask yourself the following questions: How many toes does the animal have? Are pads obvious? Do the prints have marks from toenails? How big are the prints and do they have a certain shape? Are there signs of a dragging tail? Do the paw prints appear to alternate or do they fall in a two-by-two pattern?

All these questions help the trained eye determine what animal made the print. When I see a hand-like print with five fingers, for example, I usually think of a raccoon or an opossum. By taking a closer look I can tell the difference between the two. The opossum's print will have a short thumb-like appendage and the raccoon's print will not.

If tail drag marks are present, I usually suspect a muskrat or a beaver. Most animal prints show some type of toenail. Canine tracks have large pad marks and toenails are obvious. When toenails are missing from a track, I usually think of cat-like animals. Cat prints have small pad marks and, because their toenails are so small, no toenails are seen.

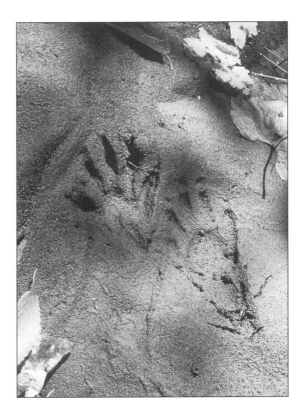

It is very difficult to tell the difference between a coyote's tracks and those of a large domestic dog. If you have the advantage of being able to follow the tracks in the snow, you might observe that the coyote inspects every bush and thicket. The domestic dog, on the other hand, generally blasts on by.

Coyotes, cats, and foxes alternate feet when they walk. Their tracks are evenly spaced and often the hind foot steps right in the track of the front foot. Raccoons, opossums, skunks, and woodchucks have an erratic walking pattern, where they just shuffle along randomly. Rabbits, squirrels, weasels, and mink hop in a two-by-two pattern. What most people don't realize when they look at the prints of a rabbit or squirrel is that the front two marks are the hind feet and the back two marks are the front feet. Squirrels hop with their front feet together while rabbits take two steps with the front feet and then hop once with the back feet.

These raccoon tracks show up particularly well in the wet sand.

Where It Lives

Where the animal lives can provide some useful hints to the animal's identity. Animals such as muskrats, beavers, ducks, geese, and snapping turtles will stay very close to a water source. Raccoons love old abandoned buildings, barns, chimneys, and hollow trees. Woodchucks, opossums, rabbits, and skunks prefer living in a hole underground but will commonly occupy a

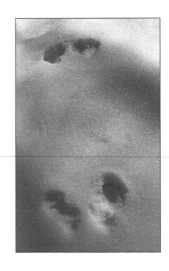

Squirrel tracks

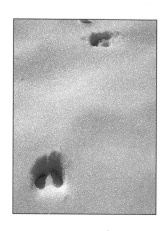

Deer tracks

space under the flooring of a shed, garage, or old abandoned building. Moles, ground squirrels, gophers, rats, chipmunks, and snakes also access their home through a hole in the ground, although the diameter of the hole is generally smaller. Larger-animal holes are approximately 6 inches (15.2 cm) wide, while smaller-animal holes average about 1 inch (2.5 cm) wide. Bats prefer the quiet, dark, stagnant air found in old caves, attic ceilings, barn roof peaks, hollow trees, and around the flashing of chimneys. Squirrels usually make nests in trees but will easily adapt to the crawl spaces in building attics, walls, and ceilings.

Deer, fox, and coyotes are free-roaming animals most of the year. For them, home is any location that provides security and close access to food. The canines will use an abandoned woodchuck hole for a short period of time in the spring as a nursery for their pups.

2

Do It Yourself or Hire a Contractor?

So you've identified the nuisance animal and decided that something needs to be done. Now what do you do? If you are somewhat knowledgeable about wildlife, you may decide to handle the situation yourself. But, if you are like many of the thousands of people each year who have a nuisance wildlife problem, you will be pulling out the yellow pages and reaching for the phone. Here are some things to consider.

Most nuisance wildlife agents are independent contractors who set their own fees. These agents charge in the neighborhood of $35 to $50 per animal. It pays to shop around for the best price. Should you decide to go with a national pest control company, the prices dramatically increase, often exceeding $100 per animal. Although these commercial contractors are usually found in the phone book, your regional Fish and Wildlife Agency should be able to direct you to nuisance wildlife agents. Many agents also advertise in local newspapers and sometimes in the phone book.

Should you catch it yourself or hire someone? No matter what you decide, have a plan and know the risks.

The advantage of going with the national pest control organization is that they will most likely have liability insurance. Nuisance wildlife agents and animal control officers charging the lesser fees may not be insured, although I know of many who are. Again, it pays to shop around and ask questions. If insurance is an issue, make sure to ask the agent if he or she is insured. This is especially important if someone is going to go up on your roof, if you have small children who could be injured, or if the agent will be working around priceless valuables that could be broken in the process of the remediation.

If you are worried about the insurance issue, but prefer to pay less money and go with an uninsured agent, I suggest drawing up a written agreement. An agreement in writing is much better than a verbal agreement, should a problem occur. In New York State, nuisance wildlife agents are required to obtain written permission from the complainant prior to setting any trap or removing nuisance wildlife from their property. My permission slip is quite simple and reads as follows:

Liability Release Form

I have requested Mr. Hershey to remove nuisance wildlife from my property. I understand that wild animals are sometimes unpredictable and will not hold Mr. Hershey responsible in the event that an animal in his trap should release an odor, damage property, or injure a person. I also agree that when an animal is captured in the trap, I will do my best to keep children and pets away.

Signed _____ Date _____ Phone _____

Quick Tip

Before you spend your hard-earned money hiring an animal control agent, do some research and don't be afraid to ask for references. Any reputable person or company will not be offended by these questions.

Another concern when hiring any animal control agent is the person's ethics. For example, if the person catches a skunk for you, will he or she release it far enough away so that it won't return in a night or so? Will the animal be handled in such a manner that the chances of it spraying are unlikely (see the skunk section in chapter 8 to find out how)? Will the animal be relocated or killed? If killed, how does the agent plan to handle the situation? I have heard a wide range of horror stories including an agent clubbing an opossum in front of little children, using pepper spray on raccoons, or releasing a pet skunk near a trap in order to collect the fee. Be suspicious of any company or person selling ultrasonic devices for birds. Although they do seem to work for bats and mice, they simply don't work for birds. Before you spend your hard-earned money, do some research and don't be afraid to ask for references. Any reputable person or company will not be offended by these questions.

Keep in mind, too, that just because a company charges a lot of money for its services doesn't necessarily mean that it is better or more reputable than other companies. This past winter, I was called to the home of an eighty-year-old woman who had seen a bat flying around in her basement. Prior to my call, she had called a large, nationally known pest control company for help. They responded to her complaint by telling her that they would set traps for the bat and come back in three weeks to see if they caught it. I was immediately suspicious when I heard that they had set a bat trap, since commercially there is no such thing. They charged her more than $200 for setting out about $20 worth of glue boards in places where, in my opinion, a bat would never go! They failed to catch the bat and that's when she called me. I told her that I was unaware of any commercial bat trap and that for $35, I would be more than happy to remove her bat the next time she saw it. The same company also offered to come back in the spring and find out where the bats were getting in. For that effort, they would charge her $500! Buyer beware, enough said.

Although these raccoons are cute, they could be infected with rabies, and show no signs of the disease. Always, wear gloves and keep small children away.

When weighing your options regarding hiring someone or doing it yourself, consider the following: If you have only one rabbit that is getting into your garden, it may be cheaper to hire someone to get rid of it. The average commercial live trap costs between $50 and $75. I currently charge around $35 per animal captured. Now if your problem is a family of five or six woodchucks, the costs of my services per animal start to add up. Buying a trap may be the smarter move, especially if you anticipate future problems. Another option is to rent a trap. I rent my traps for a month at a time for approximately half the cost of the purchase price.

Know the Risks

Before you decide to jump right in and capture that nuisance critter, consider the risks involved. Most people are aware that catching a skunk can lead to a pretty powerful stink if handled incorrectly. Imagine this scenario: You've captured a skunk in a live trap in your backyard. Your neighbors' dog runs through your yard and startles the skunk into spraying. Your neighbors' laundry is drying out on the line when the skunk sprays. If the wind is blowing in that direction, you may be faced with a pretty expensive laundry bill.

Wild animals captured in a live trap present a variety of hazards to the homeowner. These animals may appear cute and cuddly, especially to a small child. Opossums, raccoons, skunks, woodchucks, and squirrels can bite severely. Raccoons can and will reach right out and grab at you if given the opportunity. Always consider the possibility of a lawsuit should a neighbor's child or pet be bitten or injured as a result of your trapping. For this reason, I seldom use my homemade live traps. Commercially produced traps are sturdy and reliable. And no one can blame an injury on my live trap design.

I do have a garbage can trap design that I sometimes use for catching raccoons. This trap is child-proof when constructed properly. You'll find instructions for this trap in chapter 9. I have used the garbage can trap design exclusively for problem raccoons that had become trap-shy after being captured in typical commercial traps. Since such animals refuse to enter a commercial trap, building your own trap may be the only way you will ever catch them.

When selecting a trap, consider what you will do with the animal when caught and the amount of time in which you have to do it. Traps from left to right: Havahart 1079 Professional live trap, foot-hold trap, Conibear trap, and Havahart two-door trap.

A wild animal is not something to be taken lightly. The bite itself may be bad, but the potential of infection from diseases such as rabies, distemper, or mange is even worse. During the early stages of the disease, a rabid raccoon may not appear to be sick at all. An unsuspecting homeowner could release the animal without incident, only to be infected by rabies. Here's how it could happen. The animal is captured during the night. It chews on the cage, getting saliva on the wire. Rabies is transmitted through the saliva of the animal. The animal is released, it runs off, and you reset, rebait, or pack up the trap. In the process, you scratch yourself on a sharp piece of the wire cage that the animal was chewing on. Now you may be open to transmission of this virus. For this reason, handling traps with gloves and disinfecting them with bleach is important.

Not only do captured animals pose a threat to humans and pets, they can easily destroy property. Animals such as skunks, opossums, raccoons, and woodchucks will dig underneath and around the trap. Protect sod, gardens, flooring, and roofing beneath the trap with a piece of plywood. I know of a homeowner who tried to catch a raccoon on his roof. He had not considered what the animal would do when captured. As soon as the coon was caught, it proceeded to rip up all the shingles within its grasp. A costly mistake for the homeowner!

Lastly, when considering the risks of doing it yourself, make certain that what you are doing is legal. In New York State, for example, the use of a firearm within 500 feet (152.4 m) of an occupied building is illegal unless you own the building. There are restrictions on the size of the trap you can use and on the length of time an animal is allowed to stay in the trap. Releasing a captured animal may also be illegal if it is released on property other than your own.

Have a Plan

Once you have decided to take action against a nuisance critter, it's important to formulate a plan. You will need to decide if you want to relocate, repel, exclude, or destroy the animal.

If relocation is for you, start by setting up a Havahart live trap. Such a trap allows you to see what you've caught and enables you to release the animal unharmed. Havahart traps also make it easy to release nontarget animals caught by mistake. Live trapping can be more expensive and time consuming than some other methods.

If you will be live trapping the animal for later release, your success depends upon selecting the right bait. I've suggested baits for specific animals in chapter 5. With the right bait you will be more likely to catch your target animal and not attract domestic pets such as cats and dogs.

Repelling can work for some animals such as birds, bats, deer, and rabbits. But there are many repellents on the market that just don't work. Be sure to do your homework before spending your money. Chapter 8 will provide you with some repellent suggestions for the specific animal you are after. Repellents can be chemical or mechanical. Mechanical repellents include fencing, tree wrap, and scare devices. Chemical repellents could include items that smell bad, such as mothballs, or items that taste bad, such as cayenne pepper.

Exclusion is a time-consuming process and you must be very fussy if you are going to do it right. But it can be an effective way to keep nuisance animals out of your home. To ex-

Quick Tip

When considering the risks of doing it yourself, make certain that what you are doing is legal. In New York State, for example, the use of a firearm within 500 feet (152.4 m) of an occupied building is illegal unless you own the building.

clude an animal such as a bat, squirrel, or mouse from an area, first locate its entrance and exit holes. Then use hardware cloth or foam sealants to cover the holes.

In some instances, such as when a fox attacks your cat or a rat invades your pantry, killing the animal is the only effective, logical option. If you have decided that the animal should be destroyed, your options may include trapping, shooting, toxicants, or fumigants (gas bombs).

In formulating your plan, think ahead. Ask yourself, "If I set that live trap there, and I catch the animal, what will it do to my lawn, my roof, etc.?" If you are after a skunk, leave yourself enough room around the trap to cover it with a blanket. You will also want to give yourself an approach route, so that the skunk will not see you. If you plan to relocate the animal, select the release site ahead of time. Take the animal far enough away so that it won't return and be sure to release it where it won't become a nuisance for someone else. If you are going to destroy the animal, know the law. Select the most humane option available.

Lethal vs. Nonlethal Solutions: The Relocation Debate

In my experience, clients either want the nuisance animal relocated unharmed, or they want the animal destroyed. A higher percentage of my clients lean toward relocation, although this depends upon the type of animal and damage it has caused. Again, very few people want to see a raccoon hurt, but most people want mice, rats, and moles destroyed.

I can almost always think of a nonlethal solution to nuisance wildlife problems. When you read chapter 8, which describes strategies for individual animals, you will note that nonlethal strategies are listed first. These strategies do require more time and money, however. For example, it could take several days and several trips to a complainant's home to capture a woodchuck in a Havahart trap. Havahart traps are also much more expensive than traps designed to kill.

As a nuisance wildlife agent, it is my responsibility to move nuisance animals to new locations where they will not become a problem for other people. All too often, homeowners will catch a squirrel or other critter and release it in an area that is already saturated with that same type of animal. Before you know it, the released animal becomes a problem for somebody else. In New York State, it is illegal for anyone other than a nuisance wildlife agent to relocate and transport a nuisance animal away from his or her own property.

Knowing the risks of live trapping and relocating an animal is important. Ask yourself these questions prior to setting a live trap. Will small children stick their fingers into the trapped animal's cage and be bitten? Will your neighbor's dog scare that skunk in your trap? Will the animal spray? Will it turn on you when you are releasing it? If I take the animal down the road a mile (1.6 km) or so, will it come back? If I get bitten by the animal or scratched on the trap, will I need a rabies shot?

Trapping vs. Poisons, Fumigants, and Other Chemicals

The biggest advantage of using traps instead of poison is that you can always see your success. When a homeowner hires a contractor to remove a nuisance animal, it is much more satisfying if the client can see the results.

Poisons and fumigants can be very effective tools of the trade when used responsibly. Poisons are final and indiscriminant. Keep domestic animals away and safe. Also know that it is not uncommon for a poisoned animal to crawl away and die in an unreachable space such as in the flooring and walls. Dead animals will smell really bad for many days.

Fumigants, such as gas bombs, are also used with mixed results. If you see a woodchuck go down the hole just prior to setting off the bomb, you can be relatively certain that it will never come out of that hole again. I have had only moderate success by dropping a bomb down every available hole, hoping to get the animal. Too often I come back in a few days only to find that the critter had dug a couple of new holes. I never really know if I got the animal, if another moved into the area, or if the animal wasn't down the hole at all when I did the bombing. If I use a trap, I will always know the results.

Be aware that certain chemicals, even though they can be purchased over the counter in your grocery store, can kill you if mixed with other chemicals. Use extreme caution with any

repellent containing chemicals used to unclog drains or anything explosive like gasoline.

Naphthalene (moth balls) is an excellent repellent for bats and a few other critters. I can't stand the smell, so why should bats be any different? Unfortunately, to be most effective, moth balls must be used in very strong doses (see the section on bats in chapter 8). The use of naphthalene is not recommended around infants, so seek alternative solutions if young children will be in the vicinity of the application.

Know the Law

Most states have specific laws regarding how nuisance wildlife may be handled on and off of your property. It is important to know the laws in your own state prior to any removal work. In

New York State, for example, a landowner has the right to capture and kill most varieties of destructive nuisance wildlife on their own property. This would include such animals as squirrels, woodchucks, rats, mice, etc. Protected animals such as deer and beaver can be killed out of season only if you obtain a special permit from the fish and game department. In New York, a landowner cannot take a captured animal off his or her property and release it a mile (1.6 km) or so down the road.

Talk to your local game warden before taking matters into your own hands. One call could prevent embarrassment and fines.

New York has registered nuisance wildlife agents who are the only ones allowed to release animals back into the wild. These agents have located suitable sites for these animals. This prevents people from releasing an animal in a location where it may become a problem for someone else.

Animals such as coyotes may be protected in one state and not in another. Other animals, such as ducks and geese, are protected by federal laws and by specific hunting seasons. Some birds, such as the pigeon, aren't protected at all. Crows are regulated with specific hunting seasons. Birds of prey, such as hawks and owls, are protected all the time. Before taking matters into your own hands, pick up a fish and game regulations guide or talk with your local conservation officer.

Do you need a license and are you legal? Laws vary from state to state. In New York State, for example, a license is not required if you are doing this type of work on your own property. Should you decide to help out a neighbor and the animal is protected, you would be required to have a nuisance wildlife permit. To take unprotected animals such as woodchucks and red squirrels, you would not need a special permit, but would still need a hunting or trapping license. You cannot take the animal off of your property, although it can be humanely killed on your property. Most states require that you put your name and address on any trap you set. And you must check any traps you have set at least once every twenty-four hours.

If poison is in your plans, be aware that certain types must be applied by certified applicators. Every now and then I read about someone who incorrectly applies a poison and kills songbirds or fish in a stream.

Should you decide to use a firearm, make sure that you know the law. Legal shooting distances from occupied structures (500 feet [152.4 m] in New York State) apply. You cannot shoot from, on, or across a road. Some states may require written permission from landowners to shoot or trap on their property.

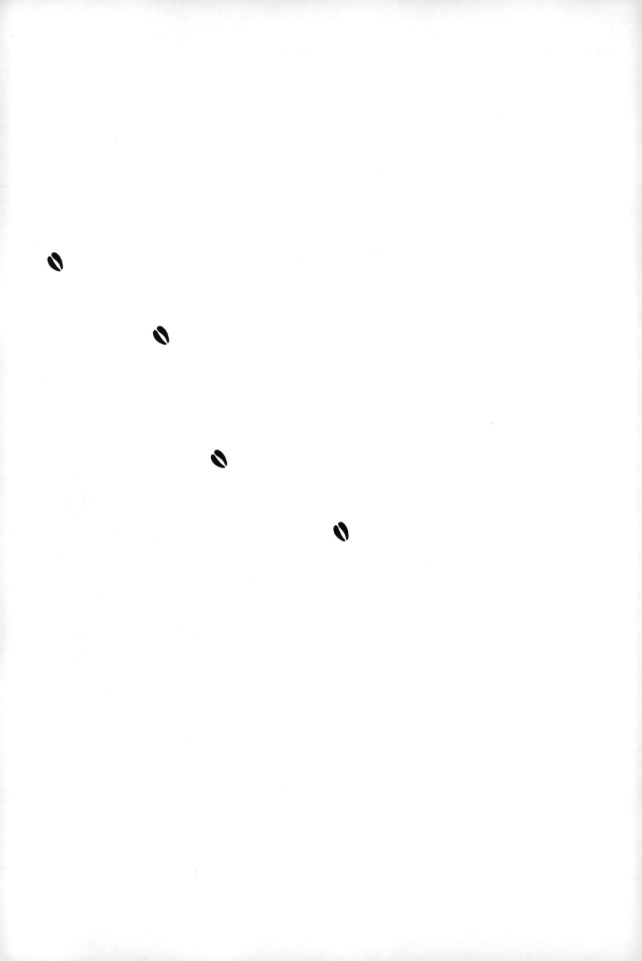

3

Deterrents

The first step in controlling a nuisance animal is to look for ways to keep the animal out of your garden, home, or yard. Deterrents are designed to block or discourage an animal's access to an area or an object. Common deterrents include fencing, tree wrap, chimney caps, grubicides, netting, and foam sealants.

Fencing

Fencing can prevent a variety of nuisance animals from raiding a homeowner's garden. Although the initial cost can be more expensive than some other deterrents, the effects are long-lasting and usually worth the investment. Fencing alone can work for rabbits, but both woodchucks and raccoons are excellent climbers. A combination of traditional fencing and electric fencing will virtually guarantee that woodchucks and raccoons will look for an alternative food source.

Electric fences, available from most farm stores, can be expensive for larger areas but are reasonably priced for the smaller garden. These fences are very effective against raccoons, woodchucks, and rabbits. But because electric fences are made with two strands of wire—one at 4 inches (10.2 cm) above ground and the other at 8 inches (20.3 cm) above the ground, deer are able to reach over them without getting zapped.

To deter deer, a fence needs to be at least 8 feet (2.4 m) tall. The most effective fence for deterring deer is 10 feet (3 m) tall; I prefer to use fences that are greater than 10 feet tall. Because

To keep deer out of an area, fencing has to be at least 8 feet (2.4 m) tall.

it contains less wire and is cheaper to produce and purchase, hog wire is usually the fencing of choice. Fence height can be reduced by slanting the fence at a 45-degree angle in the direction from which the deer are most likely to approach the fence.

Some orchards and farms are experimenting with plastic fencing. I am not at all impressed with the results so far. The fencing is not tall enough and the deer seem to be able to knock it down even when it is installed properly.

Tree Wrap

Left:
Wrap hardware cloth around a tree to protect it from voles, rabbits, and beavers. Extend the cloth into the ground and make sure it is high enough for deep snow.

To protect your favorite plantings from a variety of bark-eating animals such as deer, rabbits, beavers, and voles, wrap trees and shrubs in paper, burlap, aluminum foil, or ¼-inch (.6-cm) hardware cloth.

Each of these materials has its advantages and disadvantages. The paper material is easier and cheaper to use, while the hardware cloth lasts longer and is more durable. Always place the wrap at least 2 inches (5.1 cm) below the soil. Avoid

Center:
Wrap burlap around trees and shrubs to protect them. Repellent-treated wraps are available or you can apply repellents yourself.

Right:
Surround shrubs with hog wire to keep deer away. Plan for deep snow.

mulch if voles are your problem. You should also apply the wrap high enough on the tree or shrub to protect it in deep snow.

To protect shrubs from deer use hardware cloth, chicken wire, or hog wire to erect a circular fence around the plant. Take into account deep snows when calculating the appropriate height.

Chimney Caps

Animals seem to be attracted to chimneys. Raccoons, opossums, birds, and bats often have their young in them. Birds and squirrels sit on chimney rims. If the chimney is an outlet for the furnace, flue gases can temporarily asphyxiate the animal and they may fall down into it.

Most of the calls I have received about raccoons in a chimney involved a mother holing up there to have her young. In each case the chimney was not being used. The young are usually born on top of the fireplace damper.

I had one client who complained that a big male raccoon would climb up the side of her house, the first thing each morning. Once on the roof, it would walk up to the bathroom window and look in at her as she sat on the toilet! This completely frightened the women. After she

This is my homemade coon-proof chimney cap, made with ½-inch (1.3-cm) hardware cloth, pipe strapping, a nut, and a bolt.

screamed at it, it would run farther up on the roof and climb down the chimney, where it would spend the rest of the day. I captured this animal by fitting a chimney trap over the top of the flue tile and relocating the raccoon far enough away so that it would never bother her again. After removing the raccoon, I quickly installed a strong chimney cap. It has been my experience that once an animal's scent is there, other animals will be attracted to the chimney. With the cap installed, I had the homeowner start a big fire in the fireplace to kill any parasites or fleas and to eliminate urine and fecal odor.

Most commercial chimney caps will keep birds and squirrels from getting into the chimney. Very few are built strong enough to keep out a persistent coon or have a fine enough mesh to keep out bats. My philosophy has always been that if you are going to go through the effort of installing a chimney cap, why not install one that will keep everything out? Refer to chapter 9 for instructions on how to build your own chimney cap. My design keeps out everything from bats to raccoons and does not affect the airflow in the flue.

Grubicides

Grubicides are important to homeowners primarily because grubs (usually Japanese beetle larvae) are one of the main food sources for skunks. When skunks find grubs in the lawn, they either make small holes or tear up large pieces of sod in search of grubs. Applying a grubicide in the late spring or summer can prevent skunk damage. Get rid of the grubs and you get rid of the skunks.

A few years ago, a client called with a lawn damage complaint. The owner wanted to get rid of the skunks that were digging up her lawn. Her lawn looked like a minefield. It was littered with turned over sod and many smaller holes. There was no question she had some skunks around. The lawn had many brown spots interspersed between the nice green grass. When I explained to the woman that her lawn was infested with grubs and that's what the skunks were after, she told me that she couldn't have grubs, because she was paying a lawn service a lot of money to make sure she didn't have them. Without saying a word, I reached under the sod where there was an undug brown spot and flipped it over to reveal a very large grub. Needless to say, she immediately called her lawn service to find out what she had been paying for. I tell this story to warn homeowners to pay attention and do their homework before paying a lot of money for grubicide application. Application methods change from year to year so be sure to get a guarantee if you are hiring someone to apply it. Should you decide to apply it yourself, contact your local cooperative extension service for the latest control methods.

Japanese beetle traps are sold in many farm stores. The traps use a sexual attractant to lure the beetles into the trap. Although they do collect many beetles, I am not so sure that *attracting* them to your yard is the best idea. Killing the ones that are already there and discouraging them with grubicides is more effective.

I discovered this grub under a patch of brown sod. When skunks dig up your lawn, they are hunting for such grubs.

Netting

Netting effectively prevents birds from eating garden vegetables, strawberries, blueberries, etc. Lightweight netting can be purchased at most local farm stores. Instead of placing netting loosely over the plant, I have found that it is worth the extra effort to make a simple frame to support the netting. Birds will continue to peck at the berries if they can reach the fruit through it. Netting does not work well for squirrels or woodchucks.

Foam Sealants and Caulk

When I encounter large holes or gaps where animals may be entering a house, I generally reach for an expanding foam. Most people are familiar with my favorite sealant, Great Stuff, used to insulate around drafty windowsills, etc. It also works great for closing up holes created by squirrels, bats, mice, bees, and other nuisance wildlife. It is very messy to use, so wear gloves when applying it, and don't get it on your clothes. It goes on wet and sticky, expanding into every nook and cranny, and it dries rock-hard. It is also weather resistant and paintable.

Use foam sealants such as Great Stuff to quickly close up holes created by bees, mice, bats, and squirrels.

Use a caulking gun and good quality caulk to fill smaller holes. I use either a good latex caulk or GE Silicon II. The advantage of caulk over the foam sealant is that it comes in a variety of colors and it is easier to apply. The disadvantage of some caulks is that you can't paint over them. Before purchasing, check the label to make sure the caulk can be painted.

4

Repellents

Webster's defines a repellent as something that "drives back" or "disgusts." The use of a repellent is a good idea when you don't want to harm an animal. Repellents can scare animals away or make them stop eating your plants by giving off a disgusting smell or taste.

I break repellents into three categories: chemical, mechanical, and natural. Mothballs used in the attic to repel bats would be a good example of a chemical repellent. An electric fence installed around a garden to keep out deer, woodchucks, and raccoons is an example of a mechanical repellent. Planting marigolds around a garden is a natural repellent for rabbits. Some repellents fit into more than one category. Fox urine, for example, is a natural product of the fox, but it is mostly composed of ammonia—a chemical.

To repel deer, hang soap or bunches of human hair on tree limbs.

Some animals respond well to repellents while others do not. As with anything else, the more effort you put into repelling animals, the more successful you will be. No matter what repellent method you decide to use, you will need to stay involved in the process. Chemical repellents must be replenished after rain. Scarecrows, which are mechanical repellents, must be moved around the yard so the target animal doesn't get used to them. Natural repellents, such as marigolds, require effort, too. They must be planted, watered, and maintained. Refer to the list at the end of this chapter for the best repellents—chemical, mechanical, and natural—for the critter that's giving you trouble.

Chemical Repellents

There are three types of chemical repellents available to the homeowner to repel nuisance wildlife. Some taste bad, some smell bad, and some make the animal feel bad. Many are com-

Bad-Tasting Recipe
You can make a taste-bad repellent at home by combining 1 tablespoon (15 ml) of cooking oil, 5 tablespoons (75 ml) of cayenne pepper, and 1 gallon (3.8 l) of water. Apply this mixture to trees and shrubs to repel deer and rabbits.

mercially produced, although only about half are registered and approved by the Environmental Protection Agency.

Most of the repellents that taste bad are made from red-hot chili peppers. Homeowners apply the concoction to plants or whatever else the animal is eating. The next time the animal takes a bite, the repellent will burn its mouth. Capsaicin, a chemical found in chili peppers, is effective on voles, rabbits, and deer. It is sold by the Miller Chemical Corporation as "Hot Sauce Animal Repellent" (refer to the product manufacturer list on page 172 for for companies that sell capsaicin and other recommended repellents).

Thiram is another taste-bad repellent widely available to the public. This is a repellent that was developed for use on animals that eat bark, shrubs, twigs, etc. If used properly, Thiram is effective on squirrels, rats, mice, rabbits, pigeons, and deer.

One fairly new and promising commercially produced taste-bad repellent made especially for deer is called Hinder. Available for purchase from the Leffingwell Company, Hinder contains ammonium soaps of higher fatty acids, an ingredient deer seem to find particularly repulsive.

When hung from a shrub, plain hand soap such as Ivory will have some deer repellent properties. Some nurserymen drill a hole in a bar of soap, tie a string to it, and then hang it on the bush they want to protect.

The last two taste-bad repellents worth mentioning are called Ziram and BioMet 12. Ziram is also known as "Rabbit Scat" and can be purchased through local farm stores and from the Earl May Seed and Nursery Company. BioMet 12 is used mostly for voles and is sprayed or painted on trees.

Some repellents emit a bad smell that repels the animal. Naphthalene (mothballs), methyl nonyl ketone (crystals), putrescent whole egg solids (rotten egg), paradichlorobenzene, and tobacco dust, are all commercial examples available to the public. Naphthalene works well on bats, birds, raccoons, and skunks. Methyl nonyl ketone repels squirrels. Putrescent whole egg solids work for deer. Paradichlorobenzene repels raccoons and tobacco dust will keep rabbits away.

Sheep farmers and ranchers have been using a bad-taste device called the toxic collar to protect their livestock from canines such as coyotes and wolves. They place a collar around each sheep's neck. When the canine attacks the sheep, biting it in the neck, the bad-taste chemical in the collar will repel the attacker.

Polybutene, usually sold in the form of a sticky gel, is a type of repellent that makes the animal feel ill. When the animal steps in the gel, its feet become stuck or uncomfortable. Some polybutene products are made with an odor repellent and irritants that sting the feet. I have found a product called Tanglefoot to be very effective on roosting pigeons. Apply this sticky substance to window ledges and roof peaks with a caulking gun.

Quick Tip

Keep in mind that chemical repellents lose their effectiveness if not reapplied every four weeks and right after a rainstorm. These types of repellents should also be applied before *the damage is expected to occur.*

The effectiveness of any repellent depends on the number of critters you are trying to repel, what they are eating, and other environmental conditions. The larger the area to cover, the less effective the repellent will be.

Keep in mind that chemical repellents lose their effectiveness if not reapplied every four weeks and right after a rainstorm. These types of repellents should also be applied *before* the damage is expected to occur. It is much harder to stop the problem once it has started, than it is to prevent it from happening in the first place. Animals, especially deer, are hard to repel once they get a taste of something they really like. As deer densities increase and food supplies decrease, repellents become less effective.

A scarecrow is one of the more common types of mechanical repellents. Country dancing, anyone?

Animals respond to repellents in different ways. Some animals may not be affected by chemical repellents, some may be mildly repelled, and some can easily be repelled. Chapter 8 describes the best method available for repelling specific nuisance animals.

Mechanical Repellents
(Scare Devices)

There are all sorts of mechanical devices that can be made or purchased commercially to repel nuisance wildlife. Most of these are designed to either scare away or make life uncomfortable for the critter. The problem with most mechanical repellents is that if the same technique is used often, the animal may become used to it. To be most effective, vary the techniques.

Scarecrows are probably the most common mechanical repellent. Although used primarily to repel crows, scarecrows also work for coon, beavers, deer, canines, and rabbits. Scarecrows are most effective when moved often. Helium balloons and kites with big scary eyes are often used to keep unwanted birds, such as geese, away from sensitive areas. Recorded distress calls of the animal you want to keep away are also used on some species with good results. Bats, beavers, ducks, geese, pigeons, and seagulls will all shy away from recordings of their own kind in distress.

Scarecrow Magic
Scarecrows don't have to be scary to be effective. The key to a good scarecrow is to change its location often and try to give it some movement. Try attaching pie pans that clank in the wind to the scarecrow's arms with string. Put streamers, flags, or surveyor's tape on the arms or extended portions of your scarecrow. Most animals quickly become accustomed to new objects in the garden, so the key to success is to move the scarecrow every other day or so. Using a scarecrow in conjunction with a good repellent will double its effectiveness.

Pyrotechnic devices such as bird bangers and whistlers work quite well on geese. Before using these devices, talk it over with your neighbors, as these methods make a lot of noise. I use a handgun launcher to shoot the equivalent of an M-80 firecracker toward the geese. I try to bounce the bird bangers on the ground, about 10 feet (3 m) in front of the flock. They travel about 150 feet (45.7 m) in the air before they explode. Although I have never had this happen, I am quite sure that if the bird banger landed too close to a goose, the explosion would be lethal, so be careful. Needless to say, the geese don't stick around very long after the explosion. Bird bangers will also

scare deer out of gardens and stop a nuisance fox from chasing rabbits around the backyard. The Reed-Joseph International Company is a good place to buy a handgun launcher. (You can find Reed-Joseph's contact information in the product manufacturer list on page 172.) This company also manufactures other animal scaring devices such as carbide cannons.

Electrical devices such as electric fences and ultrasonic repellents can work for some species of animals. I have found that ultrasound works great at close distances for bats and mice, but does not work at all for large squirrels and birds.

Natural Repellents

Some naturally occurring repellents available to the homeowner are marigold plants, human hair, and some types of animal or human urine. Placing marigolds around the perimeter of the garden has proven to be an effective rabbit repellent. Growing gopher spurge plants around gardens and yards will also discourage pocket gophers. When I had trouble with deer eating my pumpkins, I went to the local barbershop and collected a bag full of hair. I placed the hair in nylon stockings and hung them around the perimeter of the patch, about 10 feet (3 m) apart. It helped! A friend of mine claims that when he hangs a rag soaked with fox urine just under his bird feeder, the squirrels will not climb up on it and eat all of the seed. Fox urine is available at most hunting stores. The rag will need to be freshened with fox urine after snow or rain.

Some animals may not be affected by chemical, mechanical, or natural repellents, some may be mildly repelled, and some can be easily repelled. Chapter 8 describes the most appropriate method available for repelling the specific animals you might encounter. The following is a quick reference list of the nuisance animals and the best repellents I have found to work.

Quick Tip

I have found that ultrasonic devices work great at close distances for bats and mice, but do not work at all for large squirrels and birds.

Animal Repellent Guide

ANIMAL	REPELLENT TYPE	TECHNIQUE
Bats	*Chemical Repellent*	Naphthalene (heavy dose), polybutenes (sticky gels applied with a caulk gun), foam sealants and caulk (not only do these deter, they give off an offensive odor to bats). I like GE Silcone II and Great Stuff.
	Mechanical Repellent	Ultrasonic devices, bright lights, wind (use an electric fan), noise—rock & roll radio playing
	Natural Repellent	Open up roost to wind and light
Beavers	*Chemical Repellent*	None available, not practical
	Mechanical Repellent	Scaring devices (electronic distress recordings, bird bangers) scarecrow, electric fences, trapping
	Natural Repellent	Draining the pond, continued removal of the dam
Bees & Wasps	*Chemical Repellent*	Citronella candles
	Mechanical Repellent	Electric fan or wind
	Natural Repellent	Change environmental conditions, watering, landscape fabrics, mulching
Deer	*Chemical Repellent*	Capsaicin, paradichlorobenzene, putrescent whole egg solids, Thiram, Ziram, Hinder
	Mechanical Repellent	Fencing (hogwire, plastic, & electric), noisemakers, scarecrow
	Natural Repellent	Human hair, chase dogs
Ducks & Geese	*Chemical Repellent*	ReJeX-iT or grape Kool-Aid mixed with water. Spray either liquid on grass where geese graze. Makes the grass taste bad to them.
	Mechanical Repellent	Scaring devices (pyrotechnics), wires strung across the water, flags, electronic distress calls
	Natural Repellent	Landscape changes (let water out of pond or change ground cover), stop feeding

Foxes & Coyotes	*Chemical Repellent*	Toxic collars on sheep
	Mechanical Repellent	Pyrotechnics, sirens, lights, scarecrow, trapping
	Natural Repellent	Human hair in bags, human urine, guard dogs, llamas
Ground Squirrels	*Chemical Repellent*	Thiram
	Mechanical Repellent	Unknown
	Natural Repellent	Fox urine on a rag
Moles	*Chemical Repellent*	Thiram, commercial grubicides (to reduce food supply)
	Mechanical Repellent	Remove grubs (mechanical devices such as noise makers and windmills don't work), trapping
	Natural Repellent	Digging out and filling in tunnels with shovel
Muskrats	*Chemical Repellent*	None available
	Mechanical Repellent	Unknown
	Natural Repellent	Eliminate food sources, drain the pond
Opossums	*Chemical Repellent*	None available
	Mechanical Repellent	Electric fencing, guard dogs, noise, trapping
	Natural Repellent	Unknown
Pigeons & Seagulls	*Chemical Repellent*	Naphthalene, polybutenes (sticky gels, i.e. Tanglefoot), Thiram
	Mechanical Repellent	Wire across window ledges and peaks, recorded distress calls, scarecrows, owl & snake decoys, shooting nearby to scare them
	Natural Repellent	Unknown
Pocket Gophers	*Chemical Repellent*	Thiram
	Mechanical Repellent	Flooding with water will drive them out (may be lethal), fencing, lead coating on wires
	Natural Repellent	Gopher spurge plant—animals avoid them, fox urine on a rag, weed control, changing soil conditions, encouraging predators

Porcupines	*Chemical Repellent*	Thiram, pentachlorophenol (on plywood)
	Mechanical Repellent	Fencing
	Natural Repellent	Unknown
Rabbits	*Chemical Repellent*	Capsaicin, naphthalene, paradichlorobezene, Thiram, tobacco dust, Ziram, blood meal
	Mechanical Repellent	Fencing, tree wrap and hardware cloth, scarecrow, colored flags
	Natural Repellent	Marigolds planted around garden, changing landscape features—mowing a big area around garden
Raccoons	*Chemical Repellent*	Naphthalene (effective only in enclosed areas), paradichlorobenzene
	Mechanical Repellent	Electric fencing, playing a radio, guard dogs, scarecrows
	Natural Repellent	Human urine
Rats & Mice	*Chemical Repellent*	Thiram, BioMet 12
	Mechanical Repellent	Ultrasonic devices (limited to one room)
	Natural Repellent	Remove weeds and debris from area, cats
Skunks	*Chemical Repellent*	Naphthalene, liquid ammonia solutions—place on a rag or in a pan
	Mechanical Repellent	Electric fencing, removing grubs, playing a radio, trapping
	Natural Repellent	Unknown
Snakes	*Chemical Repellent*	Polybutenes (glue board)—sticky substance repels or traps the snake if they go too far onto it
	Mechanical Repellent	Fencing
	Natural Repellent	Removing habitat and food supply—small rodents (mice) and amphibians (frogs)

Snapping Turtles	*Chemical Repellent*	None available
	Mechanical Repellent	Unknown
	Natural Repellent	Drain the pond
Squirrels	*Chemical Repellent*	Thiram, methyl nonyl ketone crystals
	Mechanical Repellent	Flashing around feeders and buildings
	Natural Repellent	Fox urine soaked on a rag
Voles (Field Mice)	*Chemical Repellent*	Thiram, capsaicin, BioMet 12
	Mechanical Repellent	Tree wrap and hardware cloth
	Natural Repellent	Habitat removal—mow close to trees, dig up soil with tractor; encourage predators such as hawks, owls, fox, and cats
Woodchucks (Groundhogs)	*Chemical Repellent*	Gasoline soaked rags down the hole—place while the chuck is out. May be lethal if chuck is down the hole.
	Mechanical Repellent	Electric fencing, colored flags placed at 6-foot (1.8-m) intervals, garden hose down the hole to flush them out (possibly lethal if it doesn't scare them out), scarecrow
	Natural Repellent	Unknown
Woodpeckers	*Chemical Repellent*	Tanglefoot, Roost-No-More, Bird Stop—these are all sticky substances applied where birds will step. They don't like sticky feet!
	Mechanical Repellent	Scarecrows, balloons, windmills, pie tins, owl decoys, snake decoys, kites, 2-inch (5.1-cm) aluminum strips, noise, distress calls, pyrotechniques, netting
	Natural Repellent	Removing food source—bugs

Nonlethal Solutions

There's almost always a nonlethal solution to your critter problems. Live traps, foot traps, hand capture techniques, and habitat manipulation are all humane, effective solutions and are the methods I usually recommend before any other.

Most animals—including woodchucks, raccoons, skunks, rabbits, and snakes—all respond well to my nonlethal solutions. The coyote, however, is a different story. The canine is too smart to enter a live trap, easily becomes accustomed to scare devices, and is not afraid of humans.

The biggest drawback of using nonlethal solutions is that it takes longer to see results. For example, it may take several days to lure a woodchuck into a live trap, but you can throw a smoke bomb down the animal's burrow and solve the problem in minutes.

The Havahart 1079 Professional live trap is the author's favorite.

Live Traps

The advantage of using a live trap (box trap) is that it catches the animal unharmed. The captured animal can be easily observed, relocated, and released, all with the same trap. Should you capture a nontarget animal by mistake, you can release the animal without incident. Purchase live traps from a variety of manufactures or make your own, using the tested designs I've included in chapter 9.

Manufactured live traps come in different sizes and are made by several companies. My favorite is the Havahart model 1079 professional trap, manufactured by the Woodstream

Corporation. It can be purchased through most farm stores or directly from the manufacturer (refer to the product manufacturer list on page 172 for contact information). This is a one-door model that will catch a wide range of animals from a small gray squirrel to a large raccoon. Measuring 10x12x32 inches (25.4x30.5x81.3 cm), it is an excellent coon trap, large enough to hold the really big ones. The price of a live trap increases with its size. Small traps cost between $25 and $30, while the large traps may cost as much as $80.

Havahart also makes smaller versions of their live trap for animals such as chipmunks, mice, and red squirrels. I prefer their one-door model to their two-door model, although I use both. When using the two-door models, I usually leave one door down. The only time I use the trap with both doors up is when I set it in a runway (directly in the animal's regular path), or when I know the animal is fairly small. An advantage of the two-door model is that a captured animal is much easier to release. On the two-door models, just turn the trap over and the door will flop down. One-door models have a spring-loaded door that requires using a special hook to hold the door open. This isn't difficult, but it is a little slower.

This Havahart two-door trap holds a masked bandit, waiting to be released.

If you own a two-door live trap, you will notice that the pedal to release the door is in the middle of the trap. The problem with this is that it only allows the animal to get halfway into the trap before it sets it off. If you are after a very large raccoon, the door may land on its back or tail and not completely close. When this happens, the animal can back out and get away. To prevent this, I do two things. I first make sure that I use only one door and that the closed door is securely fastened. This allows me to place the bait way back in the trap so the animal has to go farther into it. I also cut a triangular piece

Keeping a Trap Skunk-free

Skunks will eat just about anything and often wander into live traps baited for another animal. If the critter you are after is active during the day, such as a woodchuck or a rabbit, avoid catching skunks by closing the trap down just before dark and then reopening it at daybreak. Skunks are generally nocturnal, and will not be searching for food during the day.

of wood (a small rock will also work), about 3 inches (7.6 cm) long and 1 inch (2.5 cm) tall. Width is not too important. I take this wedge-shaped piece and place it under the trip pan, on the open-door side of the trap. This allows the animal to step on the front side, without anything happening. As it steps on the backside of the pan, the door closes. This trick can mean the difference between an empty trap or a captured animal.

When setting a live trap, anchor the trap to the ground. I use rope, tent stakes, ski poles, wire, or whatever I can find to make sure the animal won't tip the trap over. A smart and agitated coon can easily roll over an unanchored trap and escape.

Certain animals like raccoons and skunks will do everything possible to eat the bait without getting caught. They will try to reach into the trap from the sides, crawl on top of it, and even tip it

Here's an example of the right way to bait a trap.

over. Only when they figure out that they can't get the bait unless they go inside will they enter the trap. This is why it is so important to anchor the trap. Place the bait down the centerline of the trap and as far back as you can get it.

While we are on the subject of baiting, I always leave several bait "freebies" in front of the trap's entrance. I make a single trail, leading the animal to the large pile of bait in the back of the trap. I scatter about three pieces inside the trap near the entrance and place the rest behind the release pedal. I have found that you have to lead most animals by the nose to get them interested. Then the trick is to give them only an appetizer, not a main course. If they want the full dinner, they'll have to enter the trap. When it comes time to select the proper bait, refer to my best baits table in this chapter and you should have no problem catching that critter.

Last summer a skunk would frequent the plastic garbage bags in my garage. One particular night, I saw the skunk go

The garbage can trap is my secret weapon when trying to catch trap-shy raccoons.

Cover traps to catch rabbits and skunks. These animals prefer to enter a darker trap.

into the garage, so I quickly and quietly got a live trap, threw a can of cat food in the back, and set it so I could watch the action from my window. I learned a lot from that skunk about using baits in a trap. The skunk walked around the trap several times trying to figure out how to get at the food. It tried to reach it from the back and through the sides, but did not want to enter the trap through the open door. I didn't catch the skunk that night. The next night I took a little time and laid a trail of bait from the outside of the trap right into the trap to a larger bait pile at the back of the trap. That night the skunk started eating the bait outside and was easily led right into the trap.

When setting a live trap, place plywood underneath the trap to prevent the animal from scratching up the lawn, flooring, or your roof when it attempts to escape. Raccoons and skunks are the most notorious for doing this. Raccoons will reach out and grab anything they can get their paws on. Skunks will dig out the entire area underneath the trap.

Some animals such as coyotes and foxes are almost impossible to catch in a live trap. Canines are very smart and are extremely suspicious of anything that carries human scent. Other animals, like raccoons, may become trap-shy, and refuse to go into a trap, especially if they have had a previous encounter with one. When I am faced with a trap-shy raccoon, I get out my secret weapon—a contraption I call the garbage can trap. Plans for this trap are available in chapter 9. To the raccoon, the trap looks like a typical garbage can, complete with a free meal. But when the raccoon crawls to the bottom of the can to retrieve the food, it lands on a panel, which is connected by wire to the lid. The animal's own weight pulls the cover shut, trapping the animal securely inside. Place the trap next to a fence pole or telephone pole so that the coon can climb up the pole and then drop down into the can. Wire the handles to the pole so that the coon can't tip over the can.

Rabbits and skunks prefer to enter a darker trap. Place an old towel, tarp, or blanket over the top, back, and sides of the trap to make the space more appealing. Don't use anything of value to cover the trap because the animal will most likely pull it into the trap and destroy it.

When I'm after a rabbit or a skunk, I modify my one-door Havahart traps by fastening sheets of aluminum flashing over the top and back. This blocks the skunk's view of my approach from the rear and blocks its spray. I fasten the sheets of aluminum by first drilling holes and then securing them with plastic tie wraps.

Releasing an animal from a live trap is not that difficult if you understand how the trap operates. Although I have never had an animal turn on me as I was releasing it, I am always aware of the possibility. I always wear gloves when handling a captured animal.

To release animals such as squirrels and rabbits, point the mouth of the trap towards the woods or brush so that the animal can see it and run right for it. Stand at the opposite end of the trap, open the door, and tap the trap with your foot.

When dealing with animals that have big teeth and offer the potential of a good bite, such as raccoons or woodchucks, I place the trap under the driver's side door of my truck. I attach a long string to the trap door. To release the animal, I lean out the window of the truck and hold the door open with the string until it exits. Should the animal try to come after me, I am already in the safety of my vehicle. This is also a good way to avoid getting sprayed when releasing a skunk. Do not move when the skunk leaves the trap, especially if you are holding the door open with your hand. For some reason, skunks never seem to be in a hurry to leave a live trap. Squirrels on the other hand, shoot out like a rocket when released.

I modify the single-door Havahart, adding sheets of aluminum flashing to the top and back, so that skunks won't see me coming and spray.

No matter what kind of animal you have caught in your live trap, it is a good idea to disinfect the trap after each catch. I fill a plastic garbage can with a solution of ¼ bleach to ¾ water and dunk the trap into it. This solution does not seem to affect my capture success at all and it prevents infection. Since rabies is transmitted through saliva, you don't necessarily have to be bitten by the animal to contract the disease. If the infected animal has been chewing on the cage and you happen to scratch yourself on the wire, you could catch the disease.

The jaws of this foot trap are lined with rubber. The trap also has a special spring and swivel to prevent injury to the animal.

Quick Tip

The first rule of thumb is to use the correct size trap. Generally, a trap that catches the animal by its paw is preferable to one that reaches high on the leg.

Foot Traps (Leg-hold Traps)

Foot traps (also called leg-hold traps) can be used as either a nonlethal or lethal solution. The beauty of the foot trap is that when the right size trap is used, most animals can be released unharmed. This is especially handy if a nontarget animal gets caught in the trap. Unfortunately, the common steel leg-hold trap is the most misunderstood and misused trap available to the public. It is, when used properly, one of the most useful animal control tools available. Certain animal rights organizations have spent a great deal of time and money misrepresenting this useful tool and they continue campaigns to have this trap outlawed. All too often we hear about the young boy who incorrectly sets the trap in the middle of a trail and catches the neighbor's cat or dog. If that same boy had taken one of the many trapper education courses offered to the public, problems like this could easily be avoided.

The first rule of thumb is to use the correct size trap. Generally, a trap that catches the animal by its paw is preferable to one that reaches high on the leg. An animal caught on the paw will struggle less and will be less likely to break bones. An animal "pinched" on the pad will usually lie down and struggle very little. Laws dictate the size and type of traps that are allowed. For example, bear traps and traps with teeth cannot be used in New York State. Larger traps are only allowed underwater to trap animals such as beavers and otters. Consult your state trapping regulations guide for specific details, as laws may change annually. For most nuisance animals such as raccoons, foxes, opossums, skunks, and woodchucks, the #1½ coil spring is best. For coyotes, the slightly larger #2 coil spring is needed. For muskrat and similarly sized animals, a #1 long spring or coil spring is sufficient.

New traps come with rubber jaw inserts to prevent injury. Most are equipped with shock springs and swivels to prevent the animal from twisting its leg or dislocating a shoulder by lunging.

If used correctly, the leg-hold trap will hold the animal without injury. A number of times I have walked up to a fox caught in one of these traps to find the animal sound asleep. The properly selected trap is one that catches the animal across its pad, not way up on the leg. When the jaws of the trap snap shut on the leg, there is always more possibility for fracture. By adjusting the tension of the trap pan to a lighter setting, pad catches will be more likely. A strong pan tension, on the other hand, will cause the animal to push its foot deeper into the trap.

One of the biggest mistakes people make when setting a foot trap is that they set it in the *middle* of a hole or runway. Make sure when setting the trap that you place it to one side or the other of the centerline. Think about it—animals don't have feet in the middle of their body so why would you place the trap in the center of the hole to catch an animal by the foot? All too often people stick a trap down the hole and wonder why they have a sprung trap with chest hairs in it!

This is the right way to place a foot trap— off-center from the animal's hole or den.

By knowing the nose-to-front-foot ratio of an animal, you can be selective in what you catch, avoiding domestic pets. For example, when I am after fox, I know that the average distance from a fox's nose to its front feet is about 12 inches (30.5 cm). The average dog is about 16 inches (40.6 cm) or more. By placing the pan of the trap 12 inches from the bait, I will catch the average fox. The average dog will step up to take the bait, but not be caught. If you are setting traps with bait for smaller animals such as raccoons and woodchucks, use a 6-inch (15.2-cm) trap-to-hole ratio. If you are concerned about catching domestic animals in the foot trap, a simple solution is to make sure the animal is already down the hole and then cover the hole and

This is the wrong way to set a trap. Animals don't have feet in the middle of their bodies, so why would you set a trap in line with the center of the hole or den?

trap with a large cardboard box. Place a stone on the box to prevent domestic animals from moving it.

Unbaited traps can be as effective as baited ones. Without bait, you will have to be more of a detective, figuring out the most logical place for the animal to put its foot down. The advantage of not using bait is that you will not attract nontarget animals.

I have found foot traps most useful for capturing a squirrel in a fireplace. When this happens, I usually block off the fireplace with plywood or close the existing glass doors or screens. Squirrels will usually crawl up in the damper while I quietly place four or five set foot traps on the floor. Once placed, I close the doors, screen, or block the fireplace opening with plywood and wait until the squirrel comes down. In less than ten minutes, the squirrel will be tangled up in one of the traps. Depending on the homeowner's wishes, I then noose and relocate the critter, or destroy it. The small amount of time spent in the trap does not injure the animal. At this point, I always recommend that the homeowner invest in a chimney cap to prevent other critters from climbing down the chimney in the future.

Hand Capture: Sticks, Nooses, Glue Boards, and Gloves

Whether you are using a capture stick, a noose, a glue board, or a glove, hand capture can be a very fast way of solving a nuisance wildlife problem. I use a noose or a capture stick for the larger more dangerous animals, such as raccoons, woodchucks, and foxes. For smaller animals, such as baby raccoons, young squirrels, or opossum, a gloved hand is all that is necessary.

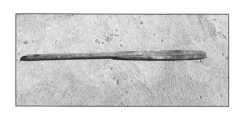

With a few modifications, an old oar makes a great capture stick for snakes. Bottom image shows the 1-inch (2.5-cm) V-shaped grove cut in the end of the paddle.

There are several commercial varieties of capture sticks available. A capture stick is simply a tube with a cabled loop on one end. To catch an animal, place the loop over the animal's head and pull the other end of the cable tight to hold the animal. Commercial capture sticks have special mechanisms that lock once you have pulled the cable tight. You can fashion your own from a piece of pipe and some electrical wire or strapping.

An old canoe paddle makes a great capture stick for snakes. I cut the paddle end off and make a 1-inch (2.5-cm) V groove in that end. The V groove is just right for garter snakes and the handle end gives you a nice grip. I slowly approach the snake with the stick and use the grooved end to pin it down. Then, while wearing gloves, I grab the snake and place it in a small garbage can.

When I have found myself in a situation where an animal the size of a woodchuck is running around inside a house, I have used a size 220 Conibear fastened to a long pole. Although a Conibear is a killer-type trap, you can modify it to hold the animal without killing it. A Conibear is essentially two wire squares with a spring attached in the middle. The animal must go through the two wire squares to be captured. To modify the trap, spread the jaws of the unset trap far enough apart to place a wood spacer on each of the four corners of the square. Make 1-inch (2.5-cm) spacers for animals the size of a squirrel, and 2-inch (5.1-cm) spacers for animals the size of a raccoon. When rigged in this manner, the trap can't clamp down too tightly on the animal. Secure the wood in place with electrical tape. Also wrap the tape around the metal jaws of the trap. I remove one of the two springs from the trap and attach the remaining spring to a pole or a broom handle with duct tape. To catch the animal, first set the trap, and then just swing the trap into the path of the running animal. Once you've caught the animal, remove it from the trap

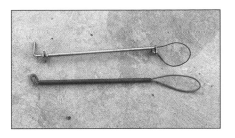

At top is a commercial capture stick with cable and cable lock device. At bottom is a homemade capture stick, made with plastic covered wire and a piece of pipe.

as soon as possible. It's stressful for the animal to remain in the trap for too long. Placing a towel around the animal's face can calm it quickly and prevent it from biting.

Sometimes, instead of placing a Conibear on the end of the pole, I attach a glue board to the pole. Purchase glue boards from the mouse trap section at your local hardware store. These boards consist of a piece of cardboard slathered with very sticky glue. This works well for smaller animals such as mice, bats, red squirrels, chipmunks, and snakes, or other animals that crawl into hard-to-reach spaces such as high ceilings and underneath stoves. To use a glue board, simply touch the board to the animal and it will become hopelessly stuck. If you plan to release the animal, put on a pair of

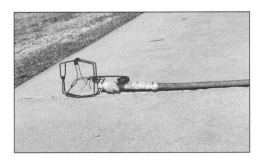

A Conibear trap duct-taped to a long pole traps fast-moving critters or those hiding in hard-to-reach places.

gloves and apply a liberal amount of vegetable oil to the glue. Slowly peel the animal from the board. Be warned that glue boards are very sticky. Aim carefully so you don't stick the board to something other than your target!

Another way to catch a problem animal is to put on a pair of gloves and just use your hands. I routinely chase down possums and pick them up by the tail with a gloved hand. I've also heard that it's quite easy to pick up a skunk by the tail, but I'm not quite ready to try that one yet. Apparently, a skunk will not spray if its feet are off the ground. If you decide to use this method, plan ahead. Have a cage nearby in which to place the captured animal.

Habitat Manipulation (Mowing and Trimming Trees)

Changing the animal's habitat and surroundings can discourage nuisance wildlife. Learn what type of habitat the animal likes and then change the habitat in your backyard so that the critter will prefer to go elsewhere. For example, if you are having problems with muskrats, beavers, or snapping turtles, consider draining your pond for a short period of time. Since all of these animals need this environment to survive, they will go elsewhere to find it.

Squirrels and raccoon can be slowed down considerably by trimming back trees so that they cannot jump onto your building. To discourage voles, avoid putting mulch around the base of your trees.

Mowing large, straight, grassy strips around gardens can give raptors such as hawks and owls a good chance at picking off animals such as rabbits, small woodchucks, and snakes. For the best results, cut strips around gardens at least 10 yards (9.1 m) across. The bigger the strip, the better, since garden raiders prefer as much cover as possible to make their approach.

Cicada killer bees thrive in very sandy soil. To get rid of cicada killer bees, you will need to change the soil conditions. Set up a lawn sprinkler, mulch the problem area, work some peat or topsoil into the sand, or put down some landscape fabric.

Best Baits

ANIMAL	BAIT
Bats	bats are not usually attracted to baits
Beavers	freshly cut poplar sprouts, commercial scents and lures
Bees & Wasps	apple juice, sugar water, beer, fruit, sodas, meat
Deer	apples, corn, pumpkins
Ducks & Geese	kernel corn, grain

Foxes & Coyotes	tainted meat, venison, skunk, rabbit, chicken, commercial scents
Ground Squirrels	walnuts, almonds, oats, barley
Moles	worms, grubs; baits are generally not effective
Muskrats	apples, carrot greens, celery sprouts, cattail roots, parsnips, oil of anise, commercial lures
Opossum	sardines, old meat, chicken entrails, bacon, cat food
Pigeons & Seagulls	bread crumbs, cereal, grains
Pocket Gophers	lettuce, carrot tops, peanut butter and molasses on whole-wheat bread
Porcupines	salt, water softener tablets, salt-soaked wood
Rabbits	apples, water softener tablets, carrots, cabbage, lettuce, red fox urine, bread (in winter); spray inside of trap with cider
Raccoons	sweet corn, bananas, cat food, marshmallows, oil of anise, bacon, sardines; fresh foods are preferred
Rats & Mice	peanut butter, birdseed, cereal, walnuts, peanuts, oatmeal, cheese, gum drops
Skunks	small white marshmallows, tainted meat, sardines, bacon, canned fish
Snakes	mice, frogs
Snapping Turtles	bloody red meat, sardines, catfish heads, carp pieces
Squirrels	peanut butter, bread, peanuts, sunflower seeds, popcorn, walnuts, almond extract on bread
Voles (Field Mice)	peanut butter, molasses, apples, corn, rabbit pellets, whole-wheat bread, oatmeal
Woodchucks (Groundhogs)	sliced bananas, apples, beans, lettuce, peas, cantaloupe, strawberries, peaches, vanilla extract
Woodpeckers	suet

6

Lethal Solutions

Lethal methods are generally used as a last resort, and only after attempts at nonlethal solutions have failed. Lethal methods should only be considered when you can be certain that nontarget animals will not be hurt. Included in this chapter are some recommendations to prevent nontarget animals from being caught. For example, to keep domestic animals out of traps, set the traps in holes and cover them with cardboard boxes. Set killer traps (Conibears) for beavers and muskrats completely underwater to prevent raccoons and other animals from being caught.

This newer style of plastic snap trap allows you to release the animal without touching it.

If you know that your nuisance animal is a furbearer, such as raccoon, fox, muskrat, or beaver, you might consider contacting a local trapper to do the job. A trapper is restricted to trapping only during the legal trapping season, when the pelts are prime or fully furred out. This is usually during November, December, and January, depending on your location. If your problem occurs during these months, you may be in luck. The trapper may do the job for free and still make a profit from the animal's pelt. The downside of using a trapper is that he or she may not want to remove all of the animals so he can come back the next year to catch some more. Reputable trappers can be located through either your state fish and game department or local trappers association.

Snap Traps

Although snap traps are commonly used to kill rats and mice, they are equally effective on chipmunks, red squirrels, weasels, and muskrats. There are many types of snap traps, but they all work more or less the same way. All snap traps consist of a flat surface and some sort of bait pan. When the animal eats the bait, it releases a spring-loaded bail (usually a wire) that snaps down on the animal. The animal usually dies quickly, but not always. A friend of mine heard some scary noises coming from her bathroom closet this summer. When she finally got the nerve to investigate, she found a deer mouse in a snap trap, caught only by the tip of its tail. She put it in a box, took it outside, and released it unharmed.

Snap traps come in two sizes: The smaller traps are just for mice, while the larger traps will catch everything from mice to moles to muskrats. These traps are among the most frequently used and probably injure more fingers than any other trap.

Hang a snap trap and you're likely to catch more mice.

There are some plastic snap traps on the market that make setting and releasing your catch much easier. By pulling the lever with your thumb, you can set the trap and release the animal without even touching the mouse (see picture on page 63).

Snap traps are also misused more than any other type of trap. All too often, a person will set the trap in the middle of the floor and wonder why they never catch anything. If a mouse does approach the trap, it has the option of approaching it from either end. When a mouse climbs on the back end of the trap to reach the bait, it just gets a ride through the air.

Attach sides to the snap trap to force the critter to approach the front of the trap.

There are several very effective ways to set a snap trap, but I have found that the most effective way is to hang the trap. For mice, I tie fishing line to the trap and hang it with a thumbtack so that the bait is about 2 inches (5.1 cm) from the floor or ledge where the mouse will be traveling. For rats, I hang it so that the bait is about 4 inches (10.2 cm) from the floor. Setting the bait holder at these heights forces the animal to stand up on its hind legs to reach the food. In this position, with its body stretched across half the trap, the mouse or rat will surely be caught when it takes the bait. Bait the traps with peanut butter, not cheese. No misses!

Two traps set back-to-back work better than one.

If you don't want to hang the trap, place the bait end of the trap tight against the wall. Setting two traps together always works better. Either set both traps side by side with the bait ends up against the wall or set the traps against the wall, end to end, with the bait ends on the outside.

It is always better to "gang set" or use more than one snap trap together. When setting this way, place the traps back to back along the edge of the wall. Baited ends should be away from each other. Put traps tight up against the wall.

Snap traps can also be used for moles and voles. Both of these critters burrow runways into your lawn. Look for rows of pushed up dirt, about 1 inch (2.5 cm) in diameter. If you find such runways in your lawn, dig out enough room to place the trap perpendicular to the runway at its base. Set the trap unbaited so that the mole or vole hits the trigger as it crawls over the trap. Place a piece of cardboard over the tunnel area to make it dark, otherwise the light-sensitive critter may shy away from the lighted tunnel. Make sure the cardboard does not obstruct the performance of the trap. (Refer to the section on moles in chapter 8 to see a picture of this trap set.)

Quick Tip

It is always better to "gang set" or use more than one snap trap together. When setting this way, place the traps back to back along the edge of the wall.

Body Gripping (Killer) Traps

Body gripping traps (also called killer traps) are spring-loaded, square-shaped traps that must be set across a tunnel opening, box, or bucket. The animal must crawl through the trap to trigger it to snap. Animals caught in this kind of trap are killed quickly. I advise against using these traps if domestic pets are a concern, but if you must use them, be sure to follow my safety tips suggested later in this chapter. I have tried a variety of these traps and feel that the Conibear manufactured by the Woodstream Corporation is the best. Trappers often call body gripping traps Conibears, even if they are manufactured by some other company.

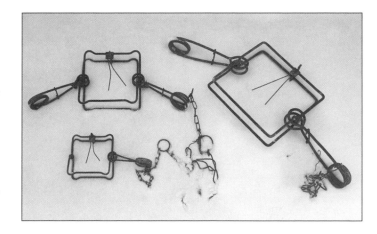

From left to right: The 110, 220, and 330 Conibear body gripping traps

Conibear traps come in several sizes. Use the 110 size for smaller animals such as squirrels, rats, and muskrats. For medium-sized animals such as woodchucks and raccoons, use the 220 size. For large animals like beaver, use a 330.

There is no need to bait a body gripping trap. Set the trap in runways, on ledges, on tree limbs, in holes in the ground, in holes under buildings, in chimneys, or any place else that the target animal may go through. Use laths or sticks to stabilize Conibears and prevent them from falling over. Place stakes either through the springs or at 45-degree angles between the two upper jaws of the trap. Always wire Conibear traps to something sturdy and use a safety catch until the trap is in position. For best results, it is smart to lightly disguise the trap profile with a few sticks or whatever natural material is in the area. Make sure not to use too many sticks, or they will affect the performance of the trap.

If you would like to use bait in conjunction with these traps, place it behind the trap, down the hole, or in the back of a box or bucket. I make Conibear boxes and buckets for both raccoons and squirrels. I cut notches in the pail or box to allow the springs to fit into the bucket. If the trap has only one spring, I use a nail or screw to fit between the jaws and stabilize the springless side. Place the bait into the back of the box or bucket. The animal must go through the trap to get the food. Boxes and buckets should be deep enough so that the animal can't reach in and get the bait without getting caught. Conibear boxes for squirrels work great on tree limbs, roofs, and gutters. Again, avoid using this type of trap, especially when using bait, if domestic pets are in the area.

With a little care, Conibears can be set around nontarget animals without catching them. Setting them underwater for beaver and muskrats will eliminate the chances of catching most domestic pets. To avoid catching ducks and other waterfowl, I float plywood over top of the trap and prop it up with sticks so that the target animal will still go into it, but a duck is unable to push its head into the trap.

To catch raccoons, opossums, or skunks on land where domestic dogs are a concern, I place a Conibear trap in a cardboard box and nail it to a tree. I use two strategically placed finishing nails to secure the 220 Conibear trap near the box's one open end, making sure the nails don't interfere with the functioning of the trap. Place the bait in the box prior to setting. Use string to tie the bait to the trap or make a bait holder using

Use laths or sticks to stabilize the body gripping trap. Set the lath between the springs at a 45-degree angle. Make sure to securely wire the trap.

Quick Tip

To avoid catching ducks and other waterfowl, I float cardboard over top of the trap and prop it up with sticks so that the target animal will still go into it, but a duck is unable to push its head into the trap.

hardware cloth or a couple of nails. I nail the prebaited box to a tree trunk about 10 inches (25.4 cm) above the ground, with the open end of the box facing the ground. The scent of the bait will lure the animal into the trap. As the animal sniffs along the ground, it will pick up the scent of the bait, look up into the trap, and get caught. Even a dog the size of a beagle will not be able to fit its head under the trap. If domestic pets are an issue, use baits such as bananas and marshmallows that will not attract domestic animals. Avoid fish and meat baits, as they are more likely to attract cats and dogs.

When using Conibears for woodchucks, I wait until I see the animal has climbed down into its burrow. Then I set a 220 trap in the hole. I use a piece of lath to stake the trap chain down securely. I then place a large cardboard box over the hole and place a rock on top to hold it down, making sure the box doesn't interfere with the movement of the trap. I do not use bait. The only time I actually put bait on the trap is when I am trapping beavers or muskrats. When trapping beavers under the ice, I wire fresh poplar sticks to one jaw, being careful not to obstruct the performance of the trap. To capture muskrats under the ice, I wire celery tops to one jaw. To trap muskrats in open water, I will sometimes put a wedge of apple on the trigger and position the bait just above the water so that the animal grabs the apple with its mouth and not its hands.

Here is an example of a Conibear trap set in a bucket. A cardboard box will work just as well.

Foot Traps (Leg-hold Traps)

As mentioned earlier, foot traps (also called leg-hold traps) can be used as either a lethal or nonlethal solution. Refer to the foot traps (leg-hold traps) section in chapter 5 for information on how to set the traps. Once the target animal enters the trap, a bullet to the brain or a blow to the head is probably the most humane way to kill the animal.

Even when you intend to kill the animal, it is important to use the correct size trap. Laws dictate the size and type of traps that are allowed. For example, bear traps and traps with teeth cannot be used in New York State. Larger traps are only allowed underwater to trap animals such as beavers and otters. Consult your state trapping regulations guide for specific details, as laws may change annually. For most nuisance animals such as raccoons, foxes, opossums, skunks, and woodchucks, the #1½ coil spring is best. For coyotes, the slightly larger #2 coil spring is needed. For muskrat and similarly sized animals, a #1 long spring or coil spring is sufficient.

I have found foot traps most useful for capturing a squirrel in a fireplace. When this happens, I usually block off the fireplace with plywood or close the existing glass doors or screens. Squirrels will usually crawl up in the damper while I quietly place four or five set foot traps on the floor. Once placed, I close the doors, screen, or plywood and wait until the squirrel comes down. In less than 10 minutes, the squirrel will be tangled up in one of the traps. If the homeowner wants me to destroy the animal, I will set larger #2 coil spring traps in the bottom of the fireplace. These traps are so large and powerful that they catch the animal by the head or body (much like a Conibear trap) and the squirrel dies quickly.

I have used the larger (coyote size) #2 coil spring traps to effectively catch and kill smaller rodents and squirrels. The larger powerful trap kills the smaller rodent quickly. I spread peanut butter on the trap pan and then sprinkle sunflower seeds on top. I set the tension of the trap pan on "hair trigger" and place the trap in the animal's travel route. Use a small screw to adjust the trap pan tension at the base of the pan. Turn clockwise to tighten and counter clockwise to set "hair trigger."

Poisons

I will say very little about poisons because I don't like using them. I usually avoid poisons because they are indiscriminant and final. With poisons, I am never quite sure how successful I have been. A poisoned animal can crawl away and die out of sight. Because people pay for my services, they often want to *see* the results.

d-CON is the most popular brand of rat and mouse poison on the market.

I do use poison to kill rodents such as rats, mice, and voles. Packets of rat and mouse poison are convenient for hard-to-reach places. You can simply toss them in. Poisons are labeled either acute or chronic. Acute poisons work in one feeding, while chronic poisons require multiple feedings to be effective. I have used an acute poison called Just One Bite with very good results. Seventy-five percent of the poisons on the market are chronic poisons. Most chronic poisons are anticoagulants, which essentially prevent the blood from clotting in the animal. The benefit to using chronic poisons is that vitamin K can be used as an antidote, should a nontarget animal get into it. The acute poisons, on the other hand, are so diverse that there may be no antidote available and death may occur after just one feeding.

Paraffin block baits work well in wet areas where cereal grain baits aren't practical. You can put a nail or screw through the wax block so the animals won't carry it away. Paraffin blocks do not become rancid, moldy, or insect ridden as cereal grain baits can. The bait is embedded within paraffin wax to keep it fresh.

When I decide to use poison and I fear that domestic or nontarget animals are in the area, I use a wood box or plastic drainpipe to make a bait station. A good box station has a 2- to 3-inch (5.1- to 7.6-cm) entry hole in each end for rats and mice. Make sure that the station is completely enclosed and that the cover has a latch so that only you and the desired critter can get to the poison. These work particularly well in chicken coops where rats are present. The Woodstream Corporation sells a commercial bait station for about $15. These come with a locking mechanism and work great if you want to keep domestic animals away from the deadly poison.

To make a poison bait station box like this one, see chapter 9.

Glue Boards

Place glue boards along walls and other places where mice and rats like to run. When the animal steps onto the board it will get stuck. Animals caught on glue boards eventually die from exhaustion. Usually by the time you find the animal in the trap it will be dead. Simply throw the dead animal and the glue board away.

Sometimes when I get a call about a squirrel in the fireplace, I use glue boards instead of foot traps. I quietly place the glue boards on the floor of the fireplace and close the doors. It doesn't take too long before the squirrel comes down to investigate and gets stuck. Once stuck, it is an easy task to grab or noose the animal and release it.

Another way to catch mice is to place glue boards right next to a wall.

Glue boards can also be effective for snakes. Every snake I have caught with a glue board has been alive when I've found it. Most of the time only the snake's head will be stuck to the board. Kill the snake by whacking it on the head with a shovel or use vegetable oil to release the snake. Place the boards in areas where snakes frequent, such as along walls, near the entrances to their holes, and on rocks or logs where they sun themselves. For large snakes, two or three glue pads attached to a plywood board works best. Put a wire or string on the board if you don't want to handle the snake when caught.

Glue boards can be used in attics for bats. I place them on windowsills, along the eaves, close to the roof peak, and near any area where the bats fly in and out.

Fumigation (Gas Bombs)

Gas bombs are not really bombs since they don't actually explode. They generally produce a smoky, sulfur-like gas, which asphyxiates the intended victim. Fumigation techniques are most effective on woodchucks and other ground animals. Do not use smoke bombs under buildings or in areas where there is dry grass as they do produce a flame, which could start a fire.

How to Gas Bomb a Woodchuck Hole

1. Watch for the woodchuck to go underground.
2. Fill a large bucket with dirt. You will use this dirt to fill in the main entrance hole after you light the fuse.
3. Use a nail to poke holes in the end of the gas cartridge.
4. Find and fill all holes with dirt except for the one you will be gassing.
5. If the soil is dry, water the hole to prevent the gases from escaping.
6. Place the fuse in the hole.
7. Light the fuse.
8. Move the bomb deeper into the hole, fuse first.
9. Cover hole with dirt from the pail.
10. Firmly stomp down the dirt.
11. If you see smoke escaping from any holes you might have missed, use a shovel to pack dirt into the holes as quickly as possible.
12. Check the hole in a few days. If it is reopened, repeat treatment.

Fumigation tends to work best when the soil in the area is watered prior to lighting the fuse, as wet soil tends to hold in the gases better. These bombs work best when used right after you actually see the animal go down the hole, otherwise you never know for sure whether or not it worked. Plug all holes except for one of the main entrance holes. The most effective time to fumigate is before the young emerge from underground in early spring.

Shooting and Hunting

Shooting nuisance animals was the traditional method of controlling critters. But as farmlands give way to development, shooting animals is becoming less and less of an option. The use of a firearm may not only be dangerous, it may be illegal. New York State law mandates that no one can discharge a firearm within 500 feet (152.4 m) of an occupied building. If you decide to use a firearm to remove a nuisance animal, make sure you are aware of your state's law.

Assuming that you can legally discharge a firearm on your property, a well placed shot with a properly sited rifle can be very effective. The advantage of shooting an animal is that you see immediate results.

I have found that some of the new high-powered pellet guns can be very effective on animals as large as a gray squirrel. Small caliber birdshot cartridges also work well. I use birdshot in my .38-caliber handgun to dispatch hard-to-reach or fast-moving snakes. It stops them in their tracks!

A good coon hound makes getting rid of that nuisance raccoon a snap.

For nighttime rats in the barnyard or corncrib, I attach a small flashlight to the end of my .22-caliber single-shot rifle. I use a .22-long-rifle birdshot and adjust the pattern so it is located in the center of my flashlight beam at about 18 feet (5.5 m). When I see a rat running across the floor, I just focus-center the beam on the rat and pull the trigger.

A henhouse-raiding fox can be lured within sight with recorded sounds of a squealing rabbit. Hunters call at night, using amplified animal sounds, a flashlight with a red lens, and a shotgun with magnum #4 shot shells. Calling at dawn and at twilight can also bring results. To call a fox, first select an ambush spot where you will be able to see the animal coming from a reasonable distance. I usually pick a hedgerow or lean up against an object like a tree to camouflage my profile. I set my tape player about 10 yards (9.1 m) out in front of me, turn it on using medium volume, and return to my ambush spot. I kneel down on one knee and keep shining the red light slowly back and forth until I see the fox's red eyes coming toward me. Then I hold the light alongside the shotgun barrel, aiming just over the fox's head and keeping the light still. The idea is to still see the reflection of the eyes as the fox approaches, but not blind the animal with the beam of light. When the fox gets to within 30 yards (27.4 m) or less I take the shot.

A designated season for hunting animals such as deer keeps the population in check.

Hunting can be used as a population control method. Raccoon hunters may be more than willing to train their dogs on the nuisance raccoon raiding your garden. Allowing deer hunting on your property can reduce the amount of ornamental shrub, crop, and plant damage. If you can prove to a state biologist that the problem is severe, wildlife management agencies may issue crop damage permits that allow you to hunt the nuisance animals during the off season. These permits are most often issued to farmers who have extreme damage to corn. State agencies may also give permits to shoot beaver if the damage or flooding is also shown to be severe.

7

Recognizing Common Wildlife Diseases

When an animal acts strangely, all too often people jump to the conclusion that the animal has rabies. Many times this isn't the case. Animals injured by automobiles, mothers protecting their young, and frightened or cornered animals can all act as if they are rabid.

Many diseases, including mange, distemper, rabies, and parasites, affect wild animals. When illness strikes, wildlife can do little to stop it. A mite infestation (mange), is not a serious problem to most domestic pets because it can be treated. However, when a wild animal is infested with mites, it suffers a terrible existence, eventually scratching itself to death.

When you encounter a suspicious animal, pay attention to detail. The more observant you are, the easier it will be to determine what is wrong. Look for bare spots or missing hair, particularly on the rump, tail, or behind the ears. Look closely at the animal's face. Are its eyes watery, or does its face appear to be wet? Is there bright red or dried blood visible anywhere? Does the animal walk abnormally? Is it dragging a leg, or its back end, or is it stumbling around? Is the animal acting aggressively or walking around as if you aren't even there?

This red fox died from a mite infestation called mange.

Homeowners should always be suspicious of any wild animal that is not afraid of them. Be suspicious of nocturnal animals that are out in the middle of the day and keep your domestic pets away from them. If your cat or dog has not had its rabies and distemper shots, make that appointment.

The coyotes in the picture appear fairly normal from a distance, but a closer look reveals hair missing on the rump of both animals. These animals were in the early stages of mange. Because coyotes are very social animals, when one member of the group becomes infested, they all get sick.

Have a plan as to what you will do if a sick animal attacks your pet. Most people rush to the aid of their pet without first protecting themselves. Avoid contact with any saliva from the bite area. Do not touch the wild animal without wearing gloves, especially if you have any open cuts on your fingers. Don't rub your nose or wipe your eyes, as these actions provide avenues through which the rabies virus can enter your body. If you are able to capture or destroy the sick animal, do not damage the head, as this is the part that will be tested. Contact your veterinarian and your local health department as soon as possible.

Mange

Mange is most often noted on canines such as the red fox, gray fox, and coyote. It can also affect domestic pets. Mange is a common name for several varieties of mites that lay their eggs under the skin of the animal. Symptoms include severe itching and loss of fur. Although mange most often infects canines, other animals, including humans, can be infected.

When looking for mange in wildlife, I look for bare or rubbed spots behind the ears, on the rump, and at the base of the tail. Sometimes the missing hair is just a small spot, other times the animal may be almost hairless.

Sarcoptic mange is probably the most familiar family of mites, but there are other types of mites that are specific to the ears and feet of animals.

Mange can be transmitted from animals to humans by a mere touch. The human form of mange is called scabies. Once, several days after touching two coyotes, I started noticing small bumps between my fingers. The bumps itched and were spread-

Below:
The legs of this red fox are are infested with mites, a condition commonly known as mange.

Below right:
Mange covers the base of this raccoon's tail.

ing fast! My doctor told me that it was scabies and prescribed a lotion called Quell. He also scolded me for touching the animals without wearing gloves.

Distemper

Distemper is a viral infection that affects both wild animals and domestic pets. There are canine and feline versions of the disease. In the wild, raccoons and foxes are the animals most likely to be affected. Symptoms include high fever, muscle twitching, diarrhea, and a discharge from the eyes and nose.

Physical signs of distemper are not as easy to see as with rabies. I can predict that an animal has distemper more by the way it acts than by the way it looks. An animal with distemper has no fear of humans and may do stupid things. They are *not* aggressive. Quite often a sick animal will walk right around humans or pets as if they aren't even there. They may crawl up on a back porch or lay down in the middle of the yard. An animal with distemper will appear disoriented and wander aimlessly. There may be some muscle twitching but the animal does not stumble, limp, or lose muscle control as an animal with rabies would.

In the later stages of the disease, an animal with distemper may seek out a stream or other water source in which to cool its body temperature. One game warden friend of mine always claimed he could find a sick fox by going to the closest water source. His theory was that the fox went to water to cool down its feverish body. Many times he would find the animal dead in the brook.

This raccoon died from canine distemper. Although there is some discharge from the eyes, the face does not look wet as it would if the animal had rabies.

Rabies

Rabies is probably one of the most feared of all wildlife diseases. It is a viral disease, usually transmitted through the bite or the saliva of an infected animal. The scariest thing about rabies is that once you have started to show symptoms of the disease, no treatment is possible. But if the victim acts fast, the disease can be cured.

If a rabid animal bites you, current medical procedures call for a series of injections around the bite area. A preventative vaccine is given immediately, followed by several more doses over a period of a month. In the past, treatment included long needles into the stomach; the injections currently used for treatment are painless. For people working with potentially rabid animals, a preventative vaccine is available. This involves three visits to your doctor over several months. The shots are injected into the arm. I have had these and they are painless. My doctor recommended the intermuscular shot over the epidermal version. The cost is about $90 per shot and all three shots are necessary.

This raccoon died from rabies. Note the wet face and the bite marks under the eye.

Several years ago, we had an outbreak of raccoon rabies in the city of Rensselaer, New York. I had the opportunity to see many sick raccoons. The most noticeable symptom on all of these animals was a wet look about the face. I have yet to see the foaming of the mouth that many cartoons have depicted over the years. Although there is no obvious foam, the animals will drool some and I suspect this is where the exaggeration comes from. The wet look is usually around the eyes and mouth.

Activity during unusual times of the day is another sign of rabies. Infected animals may also appear as if they have something in their throat. Rabies seems to be more prevalent during the spring and fall months although I have seen it pretty much throughout the year.

Aggressive behavior can also be an indicator of rabies. An animal with rabies will be very aggressive, while an animal with distemper will not be aggressive at all. Rabid animals show no fear. Coyotes, foxes, skunks, squirrels, and bats with rabies will all become very aggressive and bite at anything that gets in their way. Bite marks are often common where the animal has been fighting. All warm-blooded animals can get rabies, although I have never seen an opossum with it. Some researchers are studying the opossum to see why the marsupial doesn't seem to be affected by the virus.

In the early stages of rabies, the animal will appear perfectly normal. This is why all live-trapped animals should be considered potentially sick. Rabies is not only transmitted through the bite of an animal, it can be transmitted through an open wound, cut, or abrasion. When trapping animals, disinfect the traps and wear gloves at all times. In the later stages, the wetness of the face appears and the animal loses muscle control, usually limping or dragging itself around. The animal is also much thinner than normal.

If a suspicious animal bites you, flush the wound immediately and call your doctor. Get an accurate description of the animal. If you are able to, capture or confine the animal. If it is necessary to kill the animal, do not injure its head—the brain will be needed for testing.

Parasites

There are external and internal parasites. External parasites include bots, ticks, mites, lice, and fleas. Internal parasites include tapeworms, fluke, and roundworms.

External parasites such as the tick can cause many problems for humans. Ticks transmit two of the more common parasitic diseases: Lyme disease and Rocky Mountain spotted fever. Tick bites often go unnoticed until the telltale rash appears. Some ticks such as the deer tick are extremely small. Some are as small as the periods printed in this book. The tick's nose has many barbs. The barbs are angled so that they puncture the skin with ease but cannot be pulled out. Ticks feed on their victim's blood and can become so engorged that they may be mistaken for small tumors. Ticks can be removed with a tweezers and should be grabbed as close to the skin as pos-sible. Pull on the tick's body by twisting it in a circular motion.

A deer tick as seen on the face of a penny.

Make Your Own Flea Trap

Make a simple flea trap using a small glue board and a nightlight. Place the glue board where fleas frequent. Plug in the light bulb and hang it approximately 4 inches (10.2 cm) above the glue board. (You may need to use an extention cord.) The fleas, attracted to the warmth of the light bulb, will become hopelessly stuck on the glue.

This is the head of a dog flea as seen with an electron microscope magnified 500 times. The flea uses its long tongue to suck the blood from the victim. Flea droppings may cause skin irritation.

There is a good product on the market that combines a tweezers and a magnifying glass for removing ticks. Try to use steady upward pressure as you twist. It is important to pull the head out, so don't pull too hard or fast. If the tick head or parts of its mouth are left in, dig them out to prevent infection.

Another way of removing ticks is to completely cover them with Vaseline or grease. Ticks breathe out of their abdomen.

This is the head of a deer tick as seen with an electron microscope magnified 500 times. Note the angled barbs on the nose.

Once these air passages are blocked, they are unable to breathe and have to pull out. This method usually takes a couple of minutes and most people don't have the patience to wait. The advantage of this method is that the head comes out of the wound every time.

Mites are insects that cause mange. In humans, the infestation of mites is called scabies. These insects suck blood for their food and lay eggs under the skin, causing a serious rash. Humans and domestic pets can be easily treated for these pests, but wild animals aren't as fortunate. When infested with parasites, many of these animals die a slow, painful death.

Fleas, usually considered a pest to domestic pets, can cause problems for wild animals as well. Although rats were blamed for the spread of the plague, it was actually the flea on the rat that carried the disease. Fleas usually are very particular of the host they choose. For example there is a difference between the dog flea and the cat flea. When homeowners allow wild animals to inhabit their homes fleas can become a major problem. I know of instances where people allowed raccoons to live in their chimney or squirrels to live in their attic. The fleas multiplied rapidly and soon they lived throughout the house.

Internal parasites are not as easy to diagnose since there are no obvious external signs. Examination of the animal's stool or a postmortum autopsy may reveal either the actual parasite or the parasite's eggs. Roundworms, hookworms, and tapeworms usually attach themselves to the intestinal tract or muscular tissue, where they feed on the host animal's blood. Trichinosis and coccidiosis are some of the more common diseases associated with internal parasites.

The body of a tick expands as it sucks blood from the victim. Some ticks, such as those on this skunk, become so large that they appear to be tumors.

8

The Animals

To successfully control the critters that are giving you head-aches, you will need to know a little bit about them. On the following pages, you will find details on the twenty-eight species of wildlife most likely to wreak havoc in your yard or home. For each animal, I've included a brief life history, a description of the damage they're likely to inflict, details on how to repel them, deter them, capture them, relocate them, elimi-nate them, and recognize disease in them.

Bats

The little brown bat and the big brown bat are the two most common species of bats. Both roost in caves, hollow trees, old build-ings, chimneys, attics, and behind shutters. Bats live in colonies, mate in the fall, and have only one baby in the spring. Young bats start to fly three weeks after birth. Their pri-mary source of food is insects. Little brown

Big brown bat

bats can live to exceed thirty-four years of age. Bats are some-times called flying rodents or mice with wings, but bats are not members of the rodent family.

The Damage They Do

Bats tend to frighten people and are known carriers of rabies. Bat manure (guano) can damage vehicles and carry disease, odor, and parasites.

The bright lights that illuminate new car dealerships at-tract insects, which in turn, attract bats. Vehicle damage may occur when bat droppings fall on the new cars. If left on the surface, the urea in the bat feces eats its way through the car's paint.

Bats sometimes fly into homes when chasing an insect through an open window or door. When young bats crawl out of the roost for the first time, they sometimes get lost and end up inside of people's homes instead of outside. These young bats don't yet know how to fly and are usually mistaken for a sick animal. Roosting bats are quite noisy. Their scratching and squeaking can be objectionable. Newborn bats are particularly noisy, especially when the mother leaves them alone to search for food.

Many bats are destroyed each year by people who misunderstand them. Each case is different, but before killing one, consider the fact that one bat can eat more than a thousand mosquitoes in an hour. Contrary to popular misconceptions, bats are not blind and they do not become entangled in human hair. I suspect the reason bats come so close to humans and their hair is that they are attracted to the insects that hover around the people.

To keep bats from roosting under patio umbrellas, prop a bag of mothballs in the top of the umbrella.

Repellents

To keep bats away from your home, ultrasonic devices can be very effective if they are placed in a confined area and as close to the roosting bats as possible. Since bats can hear high frequency sounds, these devices, inaudible to humans, bombard the bat's range with jackhammer-like noise. These devices do not affect dogs or cats. Some studies have claimed that they are a waste of money, but I have found them to work quite well on both bats and mice. The trick is to place them as close to the roosting source as possible.

Persuade problem bats to relocate by creating an undesirable atmosphere. Bats don't like to roost under windy, noisy, stinky, or bright conditions. Therefore, it may be possible to drive them out by placing bright lights in the area, setting up a fan, using moth balls, and playing an all-night rock and roll station.

Umbrella Bats!

Old barns and shutters aren't the only places you'll find bats—they sometimes roost in closed-up patio umbrellas and awnings, too. To prevent this, place a bag of mothballs underneath the umbrella or in the awning before closing it up for the night. Puncture the bag or put the mothballs in a nylon stocking and tie or staple it to the inside. Bats hate the smell of mothballs and will find a more desirable place to sleep.

To create an undesirable or stinky atmosphere use large doses of naphthalene (mothballs). The odor must be strong to be effective. Do not use heavy doses of mothballs if there are small children in the house.

Deterrents

Exclusion is by far the best method of controlling bats. The best times of the year to exclude bats from an area is before mid June (before the young are born) or in early August after the young can fly. If you remove or exclude bats from an area during or after the birth of the young, the baby bats will die and the mother will be reluctant to leave.

Bat exclusion is fussy work since a bat can crawl through a hole as small as ⅝ inch (1.6 cm) wide! Placing screen or caulking over all possible entrances is the most common control method. I like using expanding foam such as Great Stuff. All exclusion work should be done at night after the bats have left the roost for their night's feeding.

When excluding bats from an area, place bat houses close to one-way valves. This will give the homeless bats an immediate home of your choosing, not theirs.

Bat Removal Hints

There are two things to keep in mind when trying to remove bats from an area: the weather and the time of year. Bats will not want to leave their comfortable surroundings if it is raining. They don't like to get wet! Reschedule your exclusion work for nicer weather and make sure to work at night, after the bats have left the roost. The worst time to try to exclude bats from their roost is when they have young that are unable to fly. The mothers will continue to enter and leave the roost, but with less frequency. Doing exclusion work when the flightless young are still in the roost will almost assuredly kill the babies. Plan to do exclusion work after August 1 to prevent this from happening.

If you can find the bat's point of entry, it is possible to set up a one-way valve to keep the bats from returning after they leave. The one-way valve is a square screen stapled over the hole. Staples are placed on the top and two sides, giving the bat just enough room to squeeze through. When the bat comes out, it hits the screen, crawls down, and flies out. When it returns, it can't figure out how to get back in. A nylon mesh funnel over the hole works in a similar way. Staple the funnel over the hole and allow it to hang several feet down the side of the building. When using either of these methods, it will take a couple of days for the bats to find a new roost. They may fly around the opening at daybreak for a couple of days, but will eventually leave. Both of these methods will work only if you have sealed all other possible entrances to the roost area, leaving the main entrance for the one-way valve. Putting up a bat house near the exit hole gives the confused bats an immediate new home and hiding place. Once they are in the bat house, the homeowner can move the bat house to a more desirable location.

Bats will sometimes hide behind old wooden shutters. When this happens, I remove the shutter and staple plastic poly sheeting on the backside. On top of the sheeting, I tape some mothballs and staple a ½-inch (1.3-cm) caulk saver (a rubber or foam tube) along the entire edge. When I replace the shutter, I caulk any remaining holes with GE Silicon II clear caulk.

Live Capture

If you have bats flying around inside your home, close off the area where the bat is flying, open a few windows, and shut off the lights. They will usually sense the air currents and fly out one of the windows. Otherwise you can easily capture a bat with a fine-mesh fishnet or coffee can. Once captured in the net, place the bat in a coffee can and release it outside.

If the bat is flying around inside the house and I can't get it in the net, I wait until it lands on a curtain, wall, or window. Then I quickly cover it with a large coffee can. Once the bat is in the can, I slide the plastic cover between the wall and the can. From this point I can release it or destroy it.

Use a badminton racket to knock a flying bat out of the air with ease. Use a fishnet if you want to release the bat unharmed. Do not use solid objects such as brooms or baseball bats. Bats can detect these objects and will avoid them.

I am not aware of any commercially made traps for bats. If you wish to trap a bat, attach a stocking or a coffee can to the end of a one-way valve placed over the primary entry point.

Lethal Methods

Sometimes more drastic measures are needed to remove a stubborn bat. Brooms and baseball bats do not work well. A badminton or tennis racket is the tool of choice. Apparently bats cannot detect the open mesh of the racket as it swings through the air. Another method of capturing bats is to buy commercially made glue boards. When the bat lands on the board's very sticky surface, it will get stuck. Once the bat is caught, simply throw out the board. The trick is to place these glue boards in strategic places—on windowsills, on ledges, behind curtains, and on roof peaks all work well. There are no registered toxicants for bats.

Best Baits
Bats cannot be lured with bait since their primary source of food is flying insects.

Handling and Relocation
No matter how you expel the bats, it is always a good idea to give them a place to go. Bat houses are a wise choice. They are available from a variety of vendors but only a few are designed with the bat's needs in mind. Most commercial bat houses are too small and don't offer enough temperature variation for the animal. A slurry of bat manure and water spread on the inside of the bat house will encourage bats to use the new home.

Host a Bat
Buying a fancy, expensive bat house and hanging it in a tree in your yard doesn't mean that bats will move right in. For best results, place the house in an open, sunny location, such as on the south or west side of a building, tree, or other structure. To attract bats to the house, you'll need to lure them away from their familiar, comfy home in a nearby attic or barn. To do so, first find a bat roost location and, wearing protective gloves, scoop up a spoonful of droppings. Add the droppings to a paper cup half filled with water. Mix the droppings and the water to make slurry. Pour this mixture into the new bat house to make it smell as if other bats have been there. Place bat houses near the exit hole of a roost, covered with a one-way valve. The bat house will give the confused and homeless bats a new place to live. When bats are roosting in the house, feel free to move the bat house to a more desirable location.

Diseases
Bats with rabies generally are found on the ground near the entrance to the roost. Sick bats can bite. If bitten by a bat, save the animal for rabies testing. Do not damage the head, as this is the part they test. If you must handle a bat, wear gloves and eye protection. Most state health departments are prepared to collect and analyze the animal in question. The good news is that less than 1 percent of the bat population is rabid. Most bats that are thought to be rabid are actually very young bats

that are just learning to fly and have lost their way. Many times these bats are found on the basement floor. A bat on the basement floor more than likely traveled through the building's exterior wall until it found an opening into the basement. These young bats may appear to be sick because they can't fly very well.

Bat guano or feces can carry disease and fungal spores. Therefore, when working near large amounts of the material, wear a respirator. Bleach is a good disinfectant and can also be used to kill the rabies virus. I use a solution of 20 parts water to 1 part bleach.

Beavers

The beaver is the largest North American rodent. Adults are reddish brown in color and weigh 35 to 50 pounds (15.9 to 22.7 kg). It has fairly small front feet compared to its very large

An adult beaver

webbed hind feet. Its tail is flat and scaly with almost no visible hair. When a beaver senses trouble, it will slap its tail like a paddle to alert other beavers of danger. The beaver has very large incisor teeth that grow continuously and become sharp as the animal gnaws on trees.

There is no way to tell a female beaver from a male beaver simply by looking at one. The beaver's favorite foods are aspen, cottonwood, willow, and pine bark. Beavers will not hesitate to eat corn from a field located close to a stream or pond. They can stay underwater for more than fifteen minutes at a time. Beavers give birth to a litter of three to four kits between March and June, and they can live to twenty-one years of age. Depending on the available food source, the average pond may have between four and eight residents.

The Damage They Do

The biggest problem with the beaver is its ability to flood roadways and large tracts of land. Beavers cut many trees and shrubs in the process of acquiring food, building a dam, and preparing a lodge. In urban areas, beavers cut or girdle trees and shrubs. They may dam drainage ditches and small streams and plug drainpipes and culverts.

Beavers are protected by environmental law, so before taking matters into your own hands, talk to your local conservation officer or game warden. If you can prove that a beaver has damaged your property, most fish and game departments will assist you with your problem and issue special kill permits.

Quite a few years ago, I worked during the summer for the State of Connecticut Wildlife Unit, relocating nuisance beaver. I learned two things: 1) a beaver can be very nasty in a suitcase live trap; 2) everybody loves a beaver until it is in their own backyard!

That summer, a local highway department was having trouble with a beaver that was flooding a town road by plugging up a culvert pipe. The landowner would not allow us nor the town to trap the beaver on her immaculately groomed estate. One day, to our surprise, we received a call from the woman. She was irate! The beaver had come out of the pond and dropped several ornamental clump birches, right by her front door. She had changed her tune and now wanted us to use dynamite to blow the so and so out of the water!

A beaver completely girdled this ornamental willow tree. The tree will die.

Repellents

No known repellents are effective on beavers.

Deterrents

One effective beaver deterrent is to use electric fencing wire across or around overflow structures. Wires should be 4 to 6 inches (10.2 to 15.2 cm) above the water level and powered by a battery. Hardware cloth around trees can help to protect them from girdling beavers. Fencing small areas such as culverts, drains, and valuable trees can be effective.

Another way to discourage a beaver from staying in the area is to destroy its dam. One caution: Before destroying any beaver dam, check with your state fish and wildlife agency; in many states, such destruction is illegal. If it is not illegal, you will probably have to remove the dam several times before the beaver gets the message. Eliminating the beaver's food supply (trees) around the pond and draining the pond in the winter can be a drastic but very effective way of telling a beaver to go elsewhere.

A typical beaver dam can block a lot of water.

Here are two ways to bait a 330 Conibear for beavers under the ice. In the top photo, I've attached the trap to a pole and baited the trap with an aspen twig. In the bottom photo, I've baited the trap with an aspen twig and hung it from a chain.

Shooting can easily frighten beaver. I use pyrotechnics called "shell crackers" to do this. They are .12-gauge shotgun shells, loaded with an M-80–like firecracker that shoots out about 75 yards (68.6 m) before it goes bang! They can be purchased from the Reed-Joseph International Corporation (refer to the product manufacturer list on page 172 for contact information). The USDA sells a scare device called the "electronic guard," a device that uses a 12-volt battery to randomly activate a combination of strobe lights and sirens. On the same principle, security lights can be installed on the dam to frighten beaver.

Live Capture

Leave live trapping and relocating beaver to your state fish and wildlife agency. In some states, it may be illegal to relocate the animal or to move it off of your property.

Lethal Methods

Trapping is the preferred method of removing a nuisance beaver. The 330 Conibear is the trap of choice, although a very strong #3 or #4 foot trap can be used under the right circumstances. I set the large foot traps on or around the beaver dam, where the animals emerge from the water. To set traps underwater, attach a heavy weight and drowning wire to the trap chain and drop the weight in deep water. Use a stake to anchor the drowning wire on the shore or dam. Thread the wire through the chain ring and place the trap where the beaver steps as it moves in and out of the water. When the beaver gets caught in the trap it will instinctively head for deep water. The wire allows the beaver to go into the deep water but will not allow it to return to the shallow water. The weight of the trap quickly drowns the beaver. Conibears don't require heavy weights and drowning wires. Set Conibears underwater in runways, culverts, narrow spots in streams, or in bank holes. This type of set is usually unbaited and must be securely fastened to the ground or some other stationary object.

The only time I bait a Conibear for beaver is under the ice. To do this, I find an aspen or poplar limb about 1 inch (2.5 cm) in diameter and notch each end to make it just fit in between one of the bottom jaws of the trap. To make it look really attractive, I take at least a dozen or so smaller aspen bud shoots off the end of a limb or two and stick them into pre-drilled holes in the approximately 1-inch (2.5-cm) diameter piece. These aspen shoots are usually about 2½ inches (6.4 cm) long and ¼ inch (.6 cm) thick. I then cut a hole in the ice where I suspect the beaver will be traveling regularly. I set the trap and lower it into the hole so that the working action of the trap is just under the ice. Then I secure the trap by putting a strong limb or pipe through the trap chain loop. The beaver swims up to the trap and holds on with its front feet. When it reaches for the bait, its head gets caught in the trap.

A good trapper can accurately tell how many animals are in a pond by the number of tracks or other animal sign in the area. Some trappers will measure the distance from the ground to teeth marks on the cut trees to see how many smaller ones are around, and also to see where the bigger ones are working. Young beaver stay very close to the lodge for the first year, so if you want to catch a lot of them, set traps close to the lodge and food pile. The wise trapper knows that the beavers with extra-large pelts will travel the farthest from the lodge, and will there-fore set traps in the outlets and inlets.

When beavers overpopulate an area or become destruc-tive, the fish and game department may issue permits to shoot them. When I am allowed to do this, I have found that using a flashlight with a red lens is effective. A beaver's eyes shine with the flashlight and you can get close enough to shoot with a shotgun. A #4 shot at about 25 yards (22.9 m) or less will do the job.

Best Baits

Fresh cut aspen or poplar branches (with lots of small bud shoots sticking out) are beavers' preferred food. If I can't find one of these branches, I make one by sticking shoots into a stick. Commercial lures and scents can work if placed behind the trap.

Handling and Relocation

Relocation and handling of beaver is best left to wildlife regu-latory agencies. Most areas suitable for beavers are already well populated, so most agencies will issue permits to shoot the beaver rather than make it a problem for someone else. Very few beaver are relocated anymore. If relocated, they will

Quick Tip

The only time I bait a Conibear for beaver is under the ice. To do this, I find an aspen or poplar limb about 1 inch (2.5 cm) in diameter and notch each end to make it just fit in between one of the bottom jaws of the trap.

need to be moved many miles away, to a completely different watershed.

Diseases

Beavers can be infected by the rabies virus, although this is not very common. Beavers do contract a parasite called giardiasis, also known as "beaver fever." This sickness can affect humans when they drink the water from a beaver flow. Symptoms include extreme diarrhea and dehydration.

Bees and Wasps

A yellow jacket nest

Most bees and wasps are social insects. The queen hibernates during the winter and begins producing eggs in the spring. They build a new nest each year, seldom using last year's model. The paper wasp usually builds its nest in trees or under the eaves of buildings. Yellow jackets usually make their nest in the ground. The honeybee, less aggressive than its cousin the yellow jacket, makes its nest in hollow trees, building walls, or in commercially prepared hives.

Yellow jackets are probably the most complained about bee of the group, although I do receive many complaints about a much larger bee called the cicada killer. Unlike the yellow jacket, the cicada killer is a very docile insect, usually about 2 ½ inches (6.4 cm) long. It is a somewhat solitary bee, although I have seen colonies of thirty to fifty of them at a time. Cicada killers tend to lay their eggs in the same sandy soil areas as the yellow jacket. Just as their name implies, they seek out grasshoppers (cicadas). They bring the paralyzed grasshopper to a predug hole and place the grasshopper in the bottom. Once at the bottom, the female lays its egg on the stunned grasshopper, which will be a food supply for the growing larva.

The Damage They Do

The biggest concern about bees and wasps is that people die each year from the sting. Many people are very allergic to bee and wasp venom.

Every so often, a queen honeybee will relocate to a new home. When the queen makes her move, the inhabitants of the hive follow her to the new location, usually a hollow log, an opening in the crotch of a tree, or sometimes even inside the walls of an old barn or house. This ball of bees, called a swarm, can be frightening to some people. When honeybees get into the walls of a home, the honey can make a real mess. I have seen bees ruin entire interior walls. The humming noise was also very disturbing to the owner.

Although ground bees don't do a lot of damage, the excavated area may be as big as a basketball. When the bees leave the nest, the area may cave in leaving a large hole in the ground. To make a nest, yellow jackets dig into the dirt, rolling the soil into tiny round balls of clay. They grab the balls with their front legs and fly out the hole, dropping the little balls 10 to 25 feet (3 to 7.6 m) away. One homeowner called me complaining that he was being pelted with tiny dirt balls that seemed to be falling out of the sky. His car was also covered with those tiny clay balls.

I recently constructed a rather large garden shed in my back yard. I made the shed out of freshly cut lumber from my brother-in-law's sawmill. Soon after the building was completed, I noticed sawdust on the front porch of the garden shed. Looking up at the rafters, I noticed several holes the size of a dime. When I looked closer, I could see the back end of a bumblebee inside each hole. The bees had dug into the wood about 4 inches (10.2 cm) deep—I am assuming to lay eggs. I killed about a dozen bees before the problem went away. They seemed to be attracted to the fresh-cut wood.

A bee bored the hole in this rafter.

Repellents

I am unaware of any repellents that are very effective on bees, although I have used citronella candles around our summer picnic table with moderate success.

Deterrents

Changing the conditions of the nesting area is the most effective way of deterring bees. Bees generally prefer to nest in hot, sunny locations. Mulching and changing the soil conditions can deter cicada killers. These large bees prefer dry, sandy soil, so I generally recommend using a water sprinkler to moisten the soil. Landscape fabrics can also discourage them from nesting in garden areas.

Yellow jackets are generally attracted to food, garbage, and fruits. They can be discouraged by keeping garbage cans closed, covering food at picnic time, and picking up fallen fruit such as apples under the tree.

Once you remove a nest from a location, seal up the area to prevent the bees from coming back the next year. Use foam sealants such as Great Stuff to quickly close up a hole.

Live Capture

Because cicada killers and bumblebees are very slow moving and few in number, you should be able to catch them with a butterfly net. Watch the bees until they fly into their shallow holes and catch them as they come out. You can either hold the net over the hole or just scoop at them as they fly from the hole.

Lethal Methods

There are also some commercial yellow jacket traps on the market and the best is made by Victor. Use a sweet bait such as apple juice or sugar water in these traps. To keep the bees from escaping, add one or two drops of liquid detergent to the water and place it at the bottom of the trap. For the best results, place several of these traps within 25 feet (7.6 m) of bee activity. Several traps are more effective than one.

Bee Careful!

Many bee sprays are good conductors of electricity, so avoid spraying the chemical at or near electrical wires or outlets! If you happen to make such a connection and are well grounded, you could get electrocuted. When buying bee spray, look for those with a dielectric breakdown voltage of 47,300 volts. These sprays do not conduct electricity and are much safer to use. Also wear gloves and avoid getting the chemical on your skin, in your eyes, or in your nose or mouth. One close friend of mine claims he had blood in his urine shortly after using a large amount of bee spray. Lastly, to make sure you get the whole nest, spray at night when the bees are all inside and groggy. If you plan to use a flashlight, place a red lens over the bulb. A red-lensed flashlight will not upset the bees as much as a normal bright white light.

To kill wasps and hornets, spray them with any of the commercial bee sprays available in stores. I have found Raid Wasp and Hornet Spray to be the best. Be careful with these types of sprays, as they can be harmful to pets. I saw what it can do to an opossum awhile ago when I responded to a complaint where an elderly women sprayed the opossum with bee spray. By the time I arrived, the animal was near death and bleeding profusely from its nose.

Spray bees at night when the entire group is on the nest. Avoid spraying during the day. You will never get all of the bees and those you do manage to spray will be much more aggressive. If you use a flashlight, don't shine the light directly on the nest, as this will wake up the bees.

Best Baits

Victor recommends using apple juice, sugar water, beer, fruit sodas, or meat as bait in their traps.

Handling and Relocation

When dealing with bees, always wear a head-net, gloves, and protective clothing. To remove a nest from an area, work at night with a red light to avoid agitating the bees. If you have a swarm of bees that needs to be moved, do not attempt to relocate the swarm yourself. Contact your local cooperative extension service for a list of professional beekeepers in your area.

Diseases

I am unaware of any diseases that can be transmitted to humans from bees. If humans are allergic to bee venom, however, a sting can be fatal. People allergic to bee stings commonly carry a prescription injection device to administer an emergency dose of epinephrine after a sting. The commercial name for this device is called an EpiPen. To keep bees at bay, the Epipen Company suggests keeping food and garbage in covered containers. Also avoid using strong-smelling hairsprays, suntan lotions, and other cosmetics or wearing bright colored clothing and flowery prints.

Quick Tip

To remove a nest from an area, work at night with a red light to avoid agitating the bees.

Deer

The whitetail deer breeds once a year and, depending on available nutrition, may produce one to three fawns in late May or June. The increased deer population means more complaints from the homeowner.

The Damage They Do

Deer are a valuable resource, but too many deer results in damage to gardens, shrubs, orchards, and motor vehicles. Wildlife

A buck in velvet

biologists are constantly looking for better ways for humans and deer to coexist. Problems with deer range from browsing on fruit tree sprouts to ruining a commercial crop of corn or pumpkins. Homeowners mostly complain about deer browsing on ornamental shrubs and trees.

When damage becomes extreme, most state wildlife agencies will issue crop damage permits (permits to shoot nuisance deer). One farmer contacted me after he had lost more than $7,000 worth of corn to the deer. I obtained a permit to kill the nuisance deer and shot twelve deer before the crop damage subsided.

Repellents

Deer repellents can be an effective but temporary solution to deer browsing. The problem with repellents is that they tend to wash off and they have to be reapplied often to protect new plant growth. I have found the least expensive and most effective deer repellent to be human hair. When deer were invading my pumpkin patch, I went to the local barbershop and brought home a bag of hair. I stuffed the hair into mesh onion bags and nylon stockings and placed them around the perimeter of

Deer Resistant Plants

The following plants and trees seem to be moderately unappealing to deer:

fir trees	weeping birch	boxwood	cactus	marigolds
spicebush	clematis	thorn apple	English ivy	iris
jasmine	juniper	honeysuckle	magnolia	daffodil
spruce trees	Scotch pine	locust	tulip	multiflora rose

the garden. I had no more problems with deer that year. Rags soaked in kerosene can also work. Resoak the rags once each month. Garden stores sell a variety of commercial products designed to repel deer—some work, some do not. Some repellents are painted on the plant to give the plant a bad taste. Others emit an odor that deer find repulsive.

When buying a commercial deer repellent, look for one containing Thiram, a chemical-tasting repellent. It was developed by the U.S. Fish and Wildlife Service and is most effective when applied to dormant plants. Although it has good weathering qualities, it must be applied often to protect the new growth of the plant. Many conservation departments use another commercial repellent called Hinder. Hinder contains ammonium soaps of higher fatty acids. It can be purchased through local farm stores or from the Leffingwell Company (refer to the product manufacturer list on page 172 for contact information). Putrescent whole egg solids and Ziram are two other repellents available to the consumer.

A hungry deer has devoured this pine tree.

Another new product that has received favorable reviews is a chemical called capsaicin. Capsaicin gets its main ingredient from hot peppers. Avoid using products having bone tar oils, as these have not been proven to be very effective. Keep in mind that under extreme overpopulation and hunger, no deer repellent will be 100 percent effective.

Deterrents

Fences or wire mesh enclosures designed to protect shrubs, trees, and gardens are the most effective exclusion methods available to the homeowner. Once installed, they are low maintenance. Deer are excellent jumpers; therefore, fences must be at least 8 feet (2.4 m) high to be effective. Electric fencing is another option. Electric fences are not difficult to install and they can be purchased from most farm stores.

Wire cages and hardware cloth can be used to protect single trees and shrubs. Place these cages far enough from the plant so that even after a significant snowfall the deer will not be able to reach the plant.

Scare devices such as barking dogs, blank shot shell cartridge explosions, or commercial noisemakers can work for a while, but deer soon learn that the danger is not real. Ultrasonic devices don't work either. There is a scare device manu-

Quick Tip

If the deer population in your area isn't too large, an effective repellent is to put a string through a bar of soap and hang it from the tree you wish to protect.

factured for the USDA called the Electronic Guard—a combination of strobe lights and sirens that go off randomly to scare the deer. If deer are attacking a smaller garden area and you can reach it with an electrical cord, think about using home security lights in place of the Electronic Guard. There is no reason that a siren or strobe light couldn't be hooked up to one of these motion detectors, too.

Some people train their dogs to chase deer. With the help of an invisible fencing system, dogs can be trained to protect only what you want protected without chasing the deer into the next county. Dogs cost less than huge fences and are not affected by snowfall.

Habitat modification can lessen deer damage. Since deer are hesitant to approach cleared areas, mowing tall grass near crops and removing nearby cover may deter them. The recreational feeding of deer can give temporary enjoyment, but can also cause long-term damage to shrubs and crops. Refrain from feeding deer. When a deer is accustomed to feeding at a location and the feeding stops, it will resort to eating anything and everything nearby. For that reason, conservation departments advise against feeding deer unless it is a long-term, continuous program.

Lethal Methods

The only lethal control method available to the homeowner is regulated hunting. All states have specific laws regarding the taking of deer, therefore, I recommend that you consult your local fish and game agency before starting an assault on your local deer population. They may offer additional solutions such as crop damage permits to shoot or at least issue harassment permits to scare nuisance deer that are a problem before or after the fall hunting season. In New York State, as in most states, a hunting license is required to hunt deer, even if it is on your property.

Diseases

Deer are known to be a host for the deer tick. This tick has now spread throughout the Northeast and elsewhere in the country and can transmit Lyme disease. Deer can also transmit rabies, but this is not very common.

Ducks and Geese

Ducks and geese can become a nuisance when they begin to overpopulate a small farm pond or graze where they shouldn't be grazing. Geese mate for life, while ducks aren't as faithful to their mates. One female duck may have several male suitors. Geese nest in the early spring of each year, but they may nest again if the eggs are eaten or disturbed. Geese lay five to nine eggs and ducks lay six to thirteen eggs. In both species, the incubation period is about twenty-eight days. The female is usually smaller than the male. It is easy to tell the sex of most ducks: The male is almost always very colorful while the female's plumage is quite dull. It is almost impossible to distinguish between the male and female goose simply by looking at them. The male goose is usually the larger one. Geese and ducks eat a variety of insects, grasses, grain, and other vegetation.

Too many geese can pollute a water source in a hurry.

The Damage They Do

Waterfowl can create a tremendous amount of damage by over-grazing grasses, trampling crops, and defecating everywhere. One goose can create a pound (.5 kg) of droppings in a day. Large numbers of waterfowl can quickly pollute a water source. Another problem with waterfowl is that once they get in the habit of going to a certain place, it is very hard to break that habit. Geese are commonly a problem at golf courses, cemeteries, reservoirs, swimming areas, airports, and on well-groomed lawns. Sometimes geese can become very aggressive and attack people. Their constant honking can be irritating, too.

Fire bird bangers from a launcher like this one.

Repellents

A commercial repellent available to the homeowner is called ReJex-It. ReJex-It is available in two formulas, one for use on land (AG-36) and one for use in the water (AP-50). The product causes the grass the birds are grazing on, or the water they are drinking, to taste bad. One friend of mine claims that a mixture of grape Kool-Aid and water sprayed on the lawn is cheaper and works great.

Ultrasonic devices do not work on birds because they can't hear them. Playing recorded bird distress calls can sometimes work. One company sells a plastic dead goose that you lay or float in the water. They claim that when geese see it, they stay away from the area.

Hanging helium-filled balloons over the pond or grazing areas is another option. These balloons have big eyes on them and can be purchased from several different vendors (refer to the product manufacturer list on page 172 for contact information). The vendors claim that one balloon will protect 5 acres (2 ha) of lawn or water.

Black flags can be used to repel waterfowl. Staple a 2x3-foot (.6x.9-m) sheet of black plastic to a pole or lath. Cut a horizontal slit in the plastic to give the flag more action when the air blows through it. Place the flags in the bird's landing and grazing areas. Reflective Mylar tape is also known to repel geese. Instead of using it as flagging, stretch the tape around the edges of ponds or other areas you'd like to keep goose-free.

My favorite method of repelling geese is to use pyrotechnics. I have used both shell crackers and bird bangers. Both devices launch an M-80–like firecracker that is designed to explode and scare the birds. Fire the shell crackers from a .12-gauge shotgun, which will launch them out about 75 yards (68.6 m). Launch the bird bangers from a handgun-like device available through Reed-Joseph International Company. These bangers travel about 50 yards (45.7 m) and then explode. The shell crackers cost about $1 each while the bangers cost about 40 cents apiece. If you have a lot of shooting to do, it's better to use the bangers.

Deterrents

Wires strung across ponds will prevent waterfowl from landing on them. Dogs can also be trained to chase and harass geese and ducks. Most importantly, do not feed waterfowl. Keeping domestic waterfowl will attract the wild variety. If you already have domestic waterfowl, your best option (other than to get rid of them) is to use the bird bangers on the wild variety. Your

Quick Tip

Black flags can be used to repel waterfowl. Staple a 2x3-foot (.6x.9-m) sheet of black plastic to a pole or lath. Cut a horizontal slit in the plastic to give the flag more action when the air blows through it.

domestic birds will probably become a little neurotic, though! Also try changing the landscape by letting the grass grow longer to make the lawn less attractive. Installing fencing between the water source and the grazing areas can also discourage geese and ducks. Finally, don't build islands in the middle of ponds if you don't want birds to nest there.

Lethal Methods

Hunting is an easy way to discourage waterfowl from making themselves at home. Quite often birds become accustomed to noisemakers and scare devices. Hunting reminds the birds that noisemakers can be dangerous.

Best Baits

Shooting waterfowl over bait is illegal.

Handling and Relocation

Fish and game laws protect waterfowl, therefore you cannot kill them outside of the normal hunting seasons. It is not illegal to scare or harass them. To successfully relocate geese you must move them more than 200 miles (321.8 km) from their nesting site or else they will find their way back. Relocation is usually not an option.

When overpopulation is a concern, you can keep the numbers under control by addling the eggs. Remove the eggs from the bird's nest and shake them vigorously for a minute or two. Mark the eggs you've addled with a pencil and place the eggs back in the nest. The bird will still sit on the eggs, but they are now infertile. If you remove the eggs, the bird will only lay more.

Foxes and Coyotes

The eastern coyote, the red fox, and the gray fox are all members of the canine family. The coyote is the largest, weighing 30 to 40 pounds (13.6 to 18.2 kg), followed by the red fox at 10 pounds (4.5 kg), and the gray fox at 8 pounds (3.6 kg). In each of these species, the male is usually larger than the female. All of the animals have similar food preferences. Mice and rabbits are foods of choice followed by birds, insects, and fruits.

The gestation period for the gray fox and the coyote is sixty-three days. The red fox gestation period is fifty-one days. Mat-

Quick Tip

When overpopulation is a concern, you can keep the numbers under control by addling the eggs. Remove the eggs from the bird's nest and shake them vigorously for a minute or two.

ing usually occurs in February and March. Foxes use dens only while they raise their four to nine young.

The gray fox is the only canine that will readily climb a tree. It prefers a brushy, thick habitat. The red fox thrives in abandoned farmland and open-field habitat. The coyote can be found just about anywhere, from the deep woods of the Adirondack Mountains to highly populated cities. Several years ago I noticed a family of coyotes living in a culvert pipe under the Empire State Plaza, South Mall Tower building in downtown Albany, New York. Of the three canines, the coyote dominates the two fox species, while the gray fox is usually more aggressive than the red fox.

Coyotes can be confused with their domestic relative, the German shepherd. One easy way to tell the difference between a coyote and a German shepherd is to look at the animal's tail. The coyote will always have a black patch at the base of the tail, and the tail will stand straight out from the body. A German shepherd's tail curls upward.

The red fox prefers abandoned farmland and is much shyer than the gray fox.

The Damage They Do

Canines attack livestock and domestic pets. Most of my complaints involve such attacks, although many people also complain that they are frightened by the coyote's or the wolf's presence and the noises it makes. The eerie howling, barking, and yipping during the night can be disturbing. One pack of coyotes near my home howls every night to the whistle of the 8:20 Amtrak train.

Canines are opportunists, taking advantage of the easiest meal. Unfortunately, that easy meal can be domestic cats, small domestic dogs, lambs, sheep, poultry, deer, and wild turkeys. Wild canines, especially the coyote, kill by attacking at the head or throat. They usually carry their meal away from the kill location. Coyotes are often blamed for damage caused by domestic dogs. Coyotes are efficient killers, bringing their prey down quickly. Domestic dogs are not efficient killers, usually attacking the victim from the rump and eating at the same location. Foxes are not as efficient at taking down larger game such as woodchucks, cats, and squirrels and may go more for the rump or anyplace else to injure, disable, and then finally kill their prey.

A Natural Repellent

Want a repellent that will love you forever? Get a dog! Dogs help keep raccoons out of the sweet corn, chase geese off of golf courses and cemeteries, are excellent mousers (i.e. the rat terrier), will alert you when an nuisance intruder nears, and will keep other canines (coyotes) a good distance away from valuable livestock.

Foxes and coyotes are nocturnal hunters, but may be seen just before dark and during the early morning hours. Animals that act strangely and are seen during the middle of the day are usually sick. Rabies is the most serious disease these animals will carry. Rabid canines will be very aggressive.

One client of mine was mowing his lawn on a riding lawn mower when a large male coyote came out of the woods. It kept trying to bite him, but he managed to dodge the animal by driving the riding mower right at it. The coyote eventually ran back into the woods. The next day a neighbor was in her above-ground swimming pool, when the same (I assume) coyote walked up the stairs to the pool, and peered down at her from the swimming pool deck. She was extremely frightened, but managed to splash enough water at it to scare it away. Six coyotes were removed from that neighborhood in the following weeks, but I never saw or caught that aggressive large male. My guess is that the animal was in the final stages of rabies and that it crawled away and died soon after that frightening day.

Repellents and Deterrents

I am aware of only one chemical repellent for canines, called Toxic Collar. Although I am not sure of the repellent's chemical make up, it is used on a collar worn by lambs and sheep. When the coyote or fox bites the animal on the neck, the canine is repelled by the collar's bad taste. The collars are expensive and there is some serious doubt that a very hungry coyote or fox will be deterred once it has acquired a taste for lamb or sheep.

Donkeys and llamas are known to be very aggressive towards canines. It may be possible to include these animals in with sheep or lambs to keep hungry canines away. Some farmers have also used trained guard dogs with some success.

There is a repellent on the market called the Electronic Guard. It is a battery operated, noisy, scaring device that uses random flashing lights and sirens to frighten predators away. It can be used in a pasture and may be purchased from Pocatello Supply Depot (refer to the product manufacturer list on page 172 for contact information). Other scare devices that can work are carbide cannons, a radio, bird banger and shell cracker-type devices, or a human-like scarecrow.

If used properly, electric fencing will deter canines. String one wire 6 inches (15.2 cm) above the ground and another wire 12 inches (30.5 cm) above the ground. Regular fencing may work, but canines are good diggers and will easily get under a poorly constructed fence. Pen up livestock, especially during the night and during the times when they are having their young. Bury dead livestock, as carrion is very attractive to canines.

I lured a red fox to this live trap with some bananas and chocolate chip cookies. It is unusual to catch a fox in this type of trap.

Live Capture

The average homeowner will have a tough time live trapping a fox or coyote. It is most unusual for one of these smart canines to enter a live or a Havahart trap. You stand a better chance catching a canine in a coil-spring leg-hold trap, or the newer rubber-jawed foot trap. These traps have specially designed springs and swivels to prevent injury. Animals caught across the pad can be transferred into a carrying cage and released without injury.

Keep in mind that catching a canine in a leg-hold trap isn't easy. Trappers must make sure the traps are scent free and properly bedded. If you are considering leg-hold trapping, contact your local trappers' association for assistance. There is quite a science to trapping the very intelligent canine. Dirt hole sets and urine post sets are most commonly used. Setting foot traps in the den of a fox or coyote may catch some of the animals, but all too often the trap-smart animal is just scared away to another location. Instead, trap the animals a short distance away from the den using a #2 or #3 coil-spring trap for coyotes and a #1½ trap for fox.

Lethal Methods

If you can find the den, fumigants or smoke bombs are an option. When the animal is down in the den, place a Conibear trap in the entrance. If the animal is outside when you set the trap, however, it will be frightened by the trap and will seek another location. Be careful with Conibear traps, as they will kill anything that can fit its head inside of them. Sometimes a den can be dug up and the animals can be physically removed, but this is best left to your local nuisance wildlife agent.

Hunting can reduce a segment of a canine population. Using hunting hounds to track the fox or coyote and attracting the fox with an electronic caller or a mouth call are two very effective methods. I have found that coyote will come running to a crow call. They are also attracted to a squealing rabbit sound, tapes of birds in distress, and a turkey call. See the shooting and hunting section in chapter 6 for more information. Since foxes and coyotes are valuable furbearers, they are regulated by state hunting seasons. Although most states allow for the taking of destructive wildlife on your own property, I would suggest consulting with your local conservation officer or regulations guide before launching your own attack.

Best Baits
Canines prefer tainted meat to fresh. They like carrion of all sorts and can be attracted by venison, skunk, rabbit, chicken, sardines, and commercial scents.

Handling and Relocation
Trapped animals are usually either noosed (then relocated) or shot at the capture site. Relocated canines must be transported at least 20 miles (32.2 km) from the capture site, but this is a job best left to the wildlife agent, especially if the canine is a coyote!

Diseases
Canines are very susceptible to rabies, mange, and distemper. An animal with rabies will appear wet around the face, may have paralysis or loss of leg movement, and will be very aggressive. The opposite is true for distemper. Most animals I have seen with distemper appear to be lethargic, stupid, and unconcerned about anything around them. An animal with distemper may walk right up to humans or lie down on someone's back porch. They tend to overheat in the final stages and may seek out a brook or lake in which to cool off before dying. Mange is actually a mite, which causes the animal to itch itself to death. In the early stages, hair loss is most common around the neck, rump, and tail.

Quick Tip

I have found that coyote will come running to a crow call. They are also attracted to a squealing rabbit sound, tapes of birds in distress, and a turkey call.

Ground Squirrels

Ground squirrels are a subset of the rodent group which includes gophers, chipmunks, prairie squirrels, Belding ground

squirrels, and rock squirrels. Ground squirrels are most active throughout the day and are true hibernators. Most are brownish yellow and may have buff-colored stripes or rows of dots down the back. Male ground squirrels breed with more than one female, but only once per year. The litter size varies from two to ten young and the animals usually live together in colonies. Ground squirrels are often seen above ground, sunning themselves and feeding. These squirrels eat a variety of foods, including insects, vegetables, seeds, other rodents, green crops, and lizards. They are active from February through October, are excellent climbers, and prefer open grassy areas such as pastures and meadows.

The chipmunk is one of the more common ground squirrels.

The Damage They Do

Ground squirrels damage gardens, farmlands, range lands, and pastures. Their holes can destroy farm equipment, injure livestock, and weaken dikes. The rodents chew on water hoses, damaging irrigation systems. Ground squirrels can cause severe destruction to forest regeneration projects by eating seeds and emerging seedlings. They also destroy fruit trees and alfalfa fields. With the exception of the Belding ground squirrel, most ground squirrels leave no conspicuous mound of dirt. Belding ground squirrels, found mostly in California, leave large mounds of dirt that can damage haying equipment. Ground squirrels are also known to prey on ground-nesting birds such as quail and ducks.

Repellents

Some people claim that mothballs will discourage squirrels. I have not found this to be true. A wildlife biologist friend of mine claims he has been able to repel squirrels by stuffing a cloth saturated with fox urine down the hole. For best results, he recommends freshening the rag about once a week. Fox urine can be purchased in most hunting stores. It is sold as a cover scent for bow hunters.

Thiram is a commercially produced repellent used to keep squirrels from chewing on vegetation. Spray or paint it on valuable shrubs. Apply often for best results.

Deterrents

Exclusion by fencing is the best deterrent. Wood fencing is preferred to wire fencing. Wood fences should be 4 to 6 feet (1.2 to 1.8 m) tall and be buried 12 inches (30.48 cm) below the ground. An electric fence attached to the wood fence provides additional security.

After removing a nuisance ground squirrel from its tunnel, the best way to discourage another invader is to rototill the area. This will remove the scent of the previous resident, which, if left, would attract any new animal to the area. If a rototiller is unavailable, seal the tunnel as tightly as possible. On a larger scale, farmers can discourage these animals by plowing the soil (deep tillage). Since these animals do not burrow very deep into the ground, plowing and rototilling can discourage a significant portion of the population.

Live Capture

To capture a ground squirrel, use the smaller-sized Havahart trap. To insure success, place traps as close to the hole as possible and use only one of the trap's doors. The best time to trap is during the month of June, when the young are just beginning to appear. Prebaiting the trap area will guarantee a catch since some squirrels may be trap-shy when the trap is first placed in the vicinity of the hole. Once the squirrel has become accustomed to eating your handouts, set the trap.

Coax ground squirrels above ground by flooding their holes with water. A garden hose down the hole will work just fine. To capture the ground squirrel, have a net, bucket, and carrying cage ready when the wet creature pops its head above ground.

Lethal Methods

Ground squirrels are nongame species, therefore, they are not protected in most states. They can be caught in large snap traps. Place the trap as close to the hole as possible. Stake the trap (in

Quick Tip

The best time to trap is during the month of June, when the young are just beginning to appear.

an upright position) to a piece of short, pointed lath. Set the baited trigger 4 to 5 inches (10.2 to 12.7 cm) above the ground so that the animal will have to stretch out its neck to get the bait. Setting the trap in this way forces the squirrel to place its head in the perfect position for the trap to snap down on it. You will catch every squirrel that goes for the bait.

Fumigants are also effective on these animals. Follow the same procedures used to fumigate woodchucks in chapter 6. Make sure to seal all entrances except one. Fumigants are not effective during hibernation.

You can asphyxiate ground squirrels by placing one end of a garden hose into the exhaust pipe of a lawn mower or motor vehicle and directing the fumes down the hole. Seal off all other entrances and place dirt around the garden hose.

Poisons are an effective way to control ground squirrels. Purchase toxic baits from your local garden or farm store. Poisons work best when you prebait the area with nontoxic food such as nuts, grain, or oats. Wait until the animals are feeding on the grain before using the toxicant. As always, keep the toxicant away from nontargeted animals by using bait stations (see chapter 9 for plans). Toxicants work best when protected from the elements. Squirrels don't like to eat moldy food any more than you do. Baits containing strychnine are restricted to below ground use in most states and may require a special permit.

Shooting can work for small populations of squirrels, but is not practical for an area that has a significant number of them. Shooting should be used as a means of controlling the survivors of other lethal methods. Check local laws about firearm usage before resorting to this method.

Quick Tip

Toxicants work best when protected from the elements. Squirrels don't like to eat moldy food any more than you do.

Best Baits
The best baits for ground squirrels are walnuts, almonds, oats, and barley.

Handling and Relocation
Relocation is not really an option with ground squirrels, mainly because most people don't want them around. In some states it is illegal to release them on public land. If you decide to relocate a squirrel, make sure you have permission to release it and are not creating a nuisance for someone else.

Diseases

Ground squirrels have fleas which in turn can carry bubonic plague. Any die-off of colonies should be reported to wildlife and health officials.

Moles

The mole is a common nuisance to many homeowners who have lawns. Moles dig tunnels close to the surface of the lawn and leave molehills wherever they go. Although there are many techniques available to get rid of moles, only a few of these methods actually work.

Moles are solitary animals, except when mating. Reproduction levels are low, so removal can be very effective. Moles spend their entire lives underground, searching for earthworms, grubs, beetles, and other insects. They are carnivores and do not eat grass, roots, or other plant parts in their search for worms and other insects. Moles tunnel through the earth extensively. They can dig a tunnel at the rate of 1 foot (.3 m) per minute. Many tunnels suggest that a lawn may have many inhabitants, but the average lawn will only have one or two. Moles have good hearing but can hardly see. They are active all year long, moving deep below the frost line during the winter. During the summer, they tunnel just under the surface of the lawn. They have a single litter of four young in late April or May.

The common mole

The Damage They Do

Moles damage lawns by digging, tunneling, and making molehills.

Repellents

There are many theories on how to get rid of moles, most of which are old wives tales that just don't work. For example, there is no evidence that castor beans, mothballs, electronic noisemakers, or vibrating windmills repel moles. Thiram is the only commercially produced repellent that is known to be effective.

Deterrents

Grubicides can make your lawn less attractive to moles by killing the grubs that they eat. If the available food supply is re-

A mole can destroy a lawn by creating mole-hills and tunnels like these.

The Victor spear trap works great on moles. Move the trap often for best results.

duced, the moles may move elsewhere. Consult your local farm store or cooperative extension service for the latest information on grubicide.

Live Capture

Digging moles out of the ground can work if you have the time and the patience. Watch the ground for new tunnel movement. If you see the soil ridging up at the beginning of a tunnel, place a shovel behind the mole and push it into a waiting bucket. Moles are most active between 4 and 7 A.M. and between 6 and 9 P.M. They are especially active after a warm rain.

Lethal Methods

Some stores sell poisoned peanuts, which work on voles (field mice), but not moles. Don't confuse the two. Moles are strict worm and grub eaters and will not be attracted to peanuts. Rumor has it that putting chewing gum down the hole will kill moles. Don't believe it! If you wish to trap the mole, commercial mole traps are available. Victor makes a good spear-type model. Do not use bait with these traps.

Trapping a mole can be tricky. The best time to trap is during the spring or after the fall rains. A day or so before you set the trap, find a couple of the tunnel's main arteries. Use your fingers to gently push the tunnel level with the surrounding ground. I say "gently" because most instructions say to push the tunnel down with your foot. This tends to compact the soil too much and discourages the mole from reusing that tunnel. Mark these pushed down tunnels so you can check the locations the next day. If moles have pushed any of these tunnels back up, you've found the right spot for the trap. To set the trap, gently push the soil back down where you had pushed it down before. To make sure there will be no obstructions when the trap is set off, push the sprung trap with spears into the ground, aligning the spears so that they are directly over the tunnel. Remove the trap from the ground and set it by pulling back on the spring and cocking the trigger mechanism. Push the set trap back into position and carefully move the trigger pedal over the runway. When the mole crawls through, it pushes up on the soil, touching the trigger to set off the trap. I have found that spear-type traps either work quickly or do not work at all. If you do not have any action, move the trap until you find an active tunnel. Often the runway that is active today will not be active tomorrow. Moles are constantly moving around, searching for worms. Moving the trap frequently is the secret to success.

Another trapping technique that can be successful is to find an active runway and dig out an area large enough to accommodate a snap-type mousetrap. Set the trap and place it on the bottom of the runway. Make sure that the trigger is at a right angle to the tunnel. Cover the hole with a board to exclude light. No bait is used, and the mole is caught as it crawls across the trap. As an alternative to the snap trap, place a glue board at the bottom of the tunnel. When the mole crawls across it, it becomes stuck.

Place snap traps and glue boards on the bottom of the tunnel. There is no need to bait the trap.

Handling and Relocation
If you wish to catch and release a mole, take it down the road a half mile (.8 km) or so and it won't come back. Moles are not extensive travelers.

Diseases
As far as I know, moles do not carry any diseases.

Muskrats
The muskrat is a valuable furbearer that lives in either bank burrows or dome-shaped houses made of vegetation (usually cattails). They are excellent swimmers, reddish brown in color, and have a 10-inch (25.4-cm) tail that is scaly and almost hairless. Muskrats weigh about 3 pounds (1.4 kg). At nine months old, muskrats breed. They have between three and six litters each year, with an average of five per litter. Muskrats start breeding as early as March. Many male muskrats die on the highways during this time of year as they are out searching for new mates. Muskrats eat mostly vegetation such as cattails and water lilies, although they will also eat freshwater mussels, crayfish, and commercial crops if the source is close to water.

The muskrat

The Damage They Do
The muskrat can cause extensive crop damage. In the Northeast, I receive many complaints about muskrats creating dan-

gerous holes along the water's edge and digging through spillways and dams. I have seen several manmade ponds where muskrats have drilled right through the dam, releasing all of the water.

Muskrats love to take up residence in a farm pond where their holes become especially dangerous to livestock, such as cows and horses. More than one valuable horse or cow has had to be put down because it broke its leg in a muskrat hole.

Muskrat holes like this one can be very dangerous to livestock.

Repellents

There are no repellents proven to be effective on muskrats.

Deterrents

One of the best ways to keep muskrats from digging into a dike, dam, or spillway is to cover the structure with large stones or hardware cloth. Usually, attempting to frighten the creature is not effective. Another way to discourage muskrats is to change the landscape, the food source, or its environment. Draining the pond over the winter months is one option. Eliminating aquatic plants may also help. Encouraging predators such as hawks, owls, and mink is a way to naturally decrease the muskrat population.

Live Capture

It's possible to catch a muskrat in live traps such as a Havahart, although they are not used too often. When muskrats are living in a bank burrow, it is sometimes possible to catch them in a stovepipe-type trap. Place the trap in the opening of the burrow, which is almost always underwater. The one-way door allows the animal to go into the trap but not come out. The stovepipe trap, made out of chicken wire, will catch multiple muskrats and, unless the upper end is allowed to stick out of the water to let the animals breathe, it will drown them. These traps are illegal in some states so check your local laws before using them.

Lethal Methods

Most muskrats are caught in foot traps or body-gripping Conibear traps. These animals are easy to catch and are considered a valuable furbearer. Conibears are most effective in runways and bank holes. Any animal that goes in or out of the hole will get caught in the trap. Multiple traps set in runways are very effective. It is fairly easy to determine which runways are active and which ones are not. If the soil on the bottom of the runway feels firm and has little silt, it is active. If it has a lot of mud, it hasn't been used in a while. Where there's a risk that a domestic duck or goose may stick its head in the trap, I cover the Conibear with a piece of cardboard.

Foot traps are most effective in areas where the animals step as they emerge from the water—on a log, on a rock, or in vegetation. Be sure to attach sufficient wire to the trap to allow the animal to swim into deeper water where it will quickly drown. Use a #1 leg-hold trap to capture muskrats.

Trapping with Conibears under the ice can be a lot of fun. I look for bubble trails leading from the edge of the bank to other parts of the pond. These trails lead from either the muskrat's feeding stations or their actual den. If it is possible to set a trap in the runway I prefer this. If the runway is too deep or not obvious I set a Conibear on a piece of lath and bait it with a celery top, a carrot top, or a piece of apple. I set the trap just under the edge of the ice, where the bubbles begin to fade out.

This Conibear trap is ready to go. To catch a muskrat, set this trap under the edge of the ice.

During warmer weather, use the same setup to catch muskrats. Place the trap along the muskrat's shoreline path with the bait trigger resting about an inch (2.5 cm) above the water line.

Snap traps can be used in this same fashion. Place a rat trap on a piece of lath, so that when set, the bait sits about 4 inches (10.2 cm) above the water. I use apples with these, and set the traps so that the muskrat must stretch its neck to get the bait.

If you can locate the dens and close off all but one hole, fumigants can work for muskrats. But beware of putting too much hope in fumigants: Muskrats often have a deep escape hole that leads into a pond.

Set snap traps attached to lath about 4 inches (10.2 cm) above the water line.

Shooting will always eliminate some of the animals but never all of them. Since muskrats are usually nocturnal, seeing them is the hardest part of hunting them. A light equipped with a red lens will not frighten the animals as much as a white light, and a shotgun with a #4 shot will do the job. Shooting over water can be dangerous so be careful of the ricochet. Some states do not allow shooting muskrats, so be sure to check with your local law enforcement agency before doing this.

Muskrats can be poisoned with anticoagulants such as d-CON, but because using poisons around farm ponds, streams, and lakes could kill fish and other aquatic life, this job is best left to the professional.

Best Baits
Apples, cattail roots, celery tops, carrot tops, oil of anise, and commercial lures are all good baits.

Handling and Relocation
Muskrats will travel long distances, especially during the mating season. If relocation is in your plans, move them to a completely different watershed, preferably more than 20 miles (32.2 km) away. Be careful when handling muskrats. For a relatively small animal, they are very aggressive. Muskrats use their sharp teeth and toenails to defend themselves.

Diseases
Muskrat diseases and parasites may include tularemia, ringworm, mites, ticks, and nematodes. Tularemia is a bacterial illness that is usually associated with rabbits. It can affect humans with symptoms including fever, chills, nausea, headache, and cough.

The opossum

Opossum
The opossum is a grayish animal with a long, hairless, rat-like tail and an uncanny ability to fake death. They are the only North American marsupial. Opossum can grow to be 33 inches (83.8 cm) long, 12 inches (30.5 cm) of which is tail. Mating occurs in the spring, when opossum give birth to five to sixteen young after a gestation period of thirteen days. Since the opossum has only thirteen nipples, only thirteen young will survive. The babies live in the mother's pouch for about three months.

The Damage They Do
Opossum are known for raiding gardens, henhouses, and garbage. When an opossum enters a henhouse, it's after either the

eggs or the chickens. They eat the eggs at the site, chewing the shells into many small pieces. Unlike raccoons, which bite the heads off the chickens before eating them, opossums maul chickens, starting at the anal opening. But the opossum—always an opportunist—doesn't limit itself to chickens and eggs. It will eat just about anything that comes along.

Look at what one of my customers found in her underwear drawer!

Opossum will nest in trees, under the ground, or just about anywhere. One unfortunate customer of mine had a small family of opossum living in her underwear drawer! The mother opossum found a way into the mobile home via a bathroom vent pipe. It climbed into the backside of my client's dresser and decided to raise its several young there.

Repellents

I know of no commercial repellents for opossum. An aggressive, barking guard dog could be used to discourage the animal in certain situations. Playing an all-night radio station in the garden might also discourage them.

Deterrents

Using fencing and hardware cloth to block off an area are the most common deterrents for the opossum. Installing an electric fence around a garden or a henhouse can be an effective way to discourage the animal. Electric fences are easy to set up and can be purchased from most farm stores.

Live Capture

Trapping opossum in Havahart box traps is one of the best ways to capture the animal. Leave live capture with foot traps for the experienced nuisance wildlife agent. If you use a box trap, be warned that you may catch skunks, as they are attracted to the same baits. Unfortunately, there is really no way to avoid this. Just set the skunk free and try again. One-

This opossum, captured in a Havahart trap, waits to be released.

door box traps work the best. My favorite is the Havahart model 1079. If you have a two-door Havahart-type trap, fix it so that only one door operates. Lift the wire of the door that you would like to make inoperable away from the pan mechanism. Place the bait way under the inoperable door. With these two-door traps, I also place a small block of wood or stone under the front part of the foot trigger. This forces the animal to go far- ther into the trap, making it is less likely that the front door will drop down on the opossum's back and allow it to back out. Always fasten the two-door models down so that the ani- mal can't roll it over and get out. To bait the trap, create a trail of food leading into the trap, placing most of the bait well be- hind the foot pedal or trigger mechanism. Entice the opossum with a few free chunks of bait, but don't give it a full-course dinner. If an opossum takes up residence in a chimney, try to trap it as close to the chimney as possible. If you place a trap on your roof, be sure to put a big enough piece of plywood underneath to prevent the opossum from ripping up your shingles once it's captured.

Lethal Methods

Trap opossum using either a Conibear trap or a foot trap. I use bucket traps for the Conibears (see the section on Conibear traps in chapter 6). There is no need to cover foot traps as opossum are not very trap-savvy and will step right onto an exposed trap. You may place both of these types of traps right into holes that the animal is using. If it is legal in your area, hunting is another option.

Best Baits

Opossums prefer tainted baits to fresh baits. I've had the most success using old meat to bait opossums. I use sardines if cats are not a concern. Opossums also go after chicken entrails, bacon, cat food, bananas, and tiny marshmallows.

Handling and Relocation

It's easy to hand capture or noose an opossum, especially when it is "playing possum" (playing dead). I wear a glove and sim- ply pick it up by the end of the tail. Once I catch it, I hold the opossum away from my body so it can't bite me; then I place it in a carrying cage. Beware that opossums don't always play possum, even when it might look like they are. They have large, sharp teeth and can be dangerous. You must be quick and care- ful when picking one up by the tail.

Opossums can bite severely so keep children and domes- tic pets away from traps. When handling a trapped animal, always wear gloves and eye protection to prevent bites and infection. If you plan to release the animal, take it at least 7 miles (11.3 km) away. Once you've caught the animal, most conservation departments have nuisance wildlife agents who can help relocate, remove, or dispose of it. If the animal must be killed, shooting it in the head with a .22-caliber rifle is the most humane method.

Quick Tip

If you plan to release the animal, take it at least 7 miles (11.3 km) away.

Diseases

Opossums can carry a variety of diseases but the most serious one is mange. Mange is actually a mite, which causes the animal to lose the fur on the back of its head, body, and tail. It can also be fatal to the opossum. In cold regions, opossums are also very susceptible to frost bite. Often pieces of their ears and the tips of their tails are missing. This should not be confused with mange.

For some unknown reason, opossum rarely get rabies. Although all warm-blooded animals are susceptible to rabies, the opossum never seem to contract it. Scientists are studying the animal to learn why and how these marsupials have developed an apparent immunity.

Pigeons and Seagulls

Pigeons are grayish birds that like to nest on window ledges, underneath highway bridges, on tall city buildings, in church belfries, and in old barns. If not controlled, these birds can quickly overpopulate an area, causing many problems for the homeowner. Pigeons lay one or two eggs that hatch in eighteen days. Peak reproduction is in the fall and spring although the birds breed all summer long.

A pigeon or rock dove

Seagulls are white birds that usually live near the ocean. As populations increase, they are seen more and more inland, especially near landfills, shopping centers, and airports. Seagulls are protected by law while pigeons are not.

The Damage They Do

People with pigeon problems complain about the bird's unsightly droppings and the cooing noises they make, usually just outside the bedroom window. Pigeons have the nasty habit of defecating all over the side of the buildings where they live. Roosting pigeons will quickly produce heaping mounds of feces, creating a real mess for the homeowner. These mounds of

Two seagulls

pigeon manure are also known to harbor many parasites, insects, and diseases. Boaters file the most complaints about seagulls. Seagulls usually perch on boat masts and booms, defecating on the inhabitants and decks below.

Repellents

It's relatively easy to keep birds from roosting, walking on, or nesting in your buildings or boat. I have had great results with a repellent called Tanglefoot, a clear, sticky, Vaseline-type product that comes in a tube. Prior to using Tanglefoot, watch the birds and note their primary travel routes and landing sites. Then use a caulking gun to apply the product to those high-traffic areas. The goo will annoy the birds and they will move to a more desirable rooftop or boat mast. Some products contain a pepper-like material that also stings the feet. I apply pepper-tainted gels in small dots or lines along the ridge top and edges of the roof. I use it in the roosting areas, on the windowsills, and anyplace else the birds frequent. It is not necessary to put it all over the roof, just apply it in the high-probability areas. The material is not cheap, but it works. I find I need about four tubes to do the average roof, less for the average boat. It takes a few days for the repellent to affect all of

How to get that bothersome bird out of your house!

Birds can enter the home in a variety of ways. An open door or window, or holes in the roof, fascia, and soffits give birds easy access. But the most common way for birds to enter a house is through the chimney or fireplace. Of course placing a chimney cap at the top of the flue would easily prevent this (see plans in chapter 9).

Once a bird is in your house, here's how to get it out. First, gather up as many bed sheets as possible and calmly cover up your valuables. I say calmly because it's important to keep the bird calm. A terrified bird can do a tremendous amount of damage to Hummels on the fireplace mantel. Then open as many windows and doors as possible to help the bird escape. You could try throwing a sheet over the bird, gathering up the bundle, and then taking it outside to let it go. A fishing net is also an option.

A neighbor once had a red-tailed hawk come crashing through his screen porch. The bird was chasing a pigeon, missed, and went right through the screen, leaving a 6-inch (15.2-cm) hole. Not wanting to tangle with its sharp beak and tallons, I used a blue tarp to construct a tunnel. I fastened the tunnel to the open door in a tent-like shape. I lifted the loose part of the tarp over the dazed bird. When it came to, it saw "the light at the end of the tunnel" and flew out the door unharmed.

the birds, and it may have to be reapplied after a few years. One drawback with this sticky repellent is that small songbirds can get stuck in the gel and die.

In addition to the repellent, I string piano or porcupine wire across window ledges, ridges, and common roosting areas. Porcupine wire is similar to barbed wire with many spike-like bristles that stick out from the main wire. Purchase the wire from vendors such as the Reed-Joseph International Company (refer to the product manufacturers list on page 172 for contact information). These fancy, high-priced, barbed wire products work fine, but I have found common piano wire to work just as well and it is more aesthetically pleasing. I start by screwing a small right-angle shelving bracket to each side of the window ledge. I position the brackets so that when I string the wire across, it will come to the belly of the bird—about 2 inches (5.1 cm) high—when the bird attempts to sit on the window ledge. If the window ledge is particularly large or there is a lot of area to cover, I will often string wires at 2 and 6 inches (5.1 and 15.2 cm) on the same window. String wires across any area that would make the ledge a less desirable place to sit.

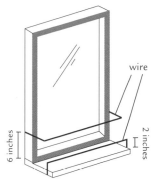

String wire across a window ledge and window to discourage pigeons from roosting there.

Two other commercial repellents, naphthalene (mothballs) and Thiram, are also effective. Both these repellents smell bad to the birds, making them want to roost elsewhere. They are both solid crystals that can be sprinkled any place the birds tend to frequent. Recorded distress calls can have some affect, but often the birds become accustomed to them. Ultrasonic devices do not work for pigeons or seagulls because they can't hear them. Scare devices such as exploding shotgun shells and carbide cannons are frequently used by farmers, but are not practical for the average homeowner. If noisemakers are an option for you, I would recommend using the launcher and shell crackers produced by the Reed-Joseph International Company (refer to the product manufacturers list on page 172 for contact information).

Deterrents

If you can reach the nest of the nuisance bird, destroying it is a smart option. Birds that are born on your property will usually return to that general area even if disturbed. Destroying the nest may just push the bird across the property line to your neighbor's window ledge. When wildlife agencies want to control duck, goose, and swan populations, they will sometimes addle the eggs. Wait until the nest is full of eggs and the mother is sitting on them and then scare the mother from the nest. Mark each egg with a pencil or permanent marker, shake it vigorously for about ten seconds, and then put it back in the nest. Addling prevents the embryos from developing and keeps the pigeon or seagull occupied, sitting on infertile eggs. Marking the eggs simply helps you remember which eggs have been addled and, upon later inspection, helps you to determine if any additional eggs have been laid.

Bird droppings can create a real mess for the homeowner.

You can exclude birds from an area by using ¾-inch (1.9-cm) hardware cloth. You may also use plastic bird meshing, but it is not as durable. If birds are roosting on window ledges, tilting the angle of the ledge to 45 degrees will make the birds more uncomfortable. Simply nail a piece of wood on top of the existing ledge. Metal flashing will work equally well.

Setting up raptor perches for birds such as falcons or red-tailed hawks can keep pigeon numbers down. These birds of prey commonly enjoy pigeon for dinner. I have a friend who is a falconer. He uses his raptors to get rid of nuisance pigeons in various barns in the Albany, New York, area. He suggests contacting your local falconers' association if you feel this may be a viable option for you. He is reluctant to use his birds of prey near highways and other high traffic areas. His concern is that when his raptor knocks the pigeon to the ground or street, his specially trained bird could become injured by a passing motor vehicle.

Live Capture

Seagulls cannot be trapped, because they are protected by law. But live trapping a pigeon is not difficult and is effective when used in conjunction with repellents. Pigeon traps can be purchased from vendors such as the Woodstream Company (refer to the product manufacturer list on page 172 for contact information). Prior to setting a pigeon trap, I recommend prebaiting the area for a couple of days. Breadcrumbs, cereal, and grain all work well. Pigeon traps are designed to catch more than one bird at a time, so when you catch the first bird, leave it in the trap to attract more birds.

Hand capturing pigeons at night can be a very successful

method. Under the cover of darkness, use a flashlight with a red lens and a long-handled fishnet. Shine the light in the bird's eyes and then swoop the pigeon up with the fishnet. Place the bird in the holding cage.

Lethal Methods

There is not a lethal method for birds available to the home-owner acting alone. Pellet guns and other firearms are an option, but should be left to the experienced nuisance wildlife agent. Avoid using poison grains because they will also affect songbirds. Remember that seagulls are protected by law and cannot be killed.

Best Baits

Breadcrumbs, cereal, and grain are all good baits for attracting pigeons and seagulls.

Handling and Relocation

Relocating trapped pigeons will not work. These birds are capable of returning to a familiar nesting spot from as far as 300 miles (482.7 km).

Diseases

When cleaning up bird manure, wear eye protection and a mask. The manure can carry fungal spores, bacteria, and parasites that could make you sick. Disinfect the area with a mild solution of bleach. Remember that bleach stains certain surfaces. Always test an out-of-sight spot before bleaching the whole area.

Birds carry a variety of parasites such as mites and lice. When birds nest near windows, these small pests can find their way into homes and bedding.

Pocket Gophers

There are six species of the pocket gopher in the United States. The plains pocket gopher is the most common. These rodents range from 6 to 12 inches (15.2 to 30.5 cm) in length. They are either dark or pale brown and, as the name implies, they have a pocket on the outside of each cheek. The critters use the pouch to carry food. The 2- to 3-inch (5.1- to 7.6-cm) tail is almost hairless. Pocket gophers are active day and night, all year long.

Pocket gophers are usually found west of the Mississippi River. People in the eastern United States should consider themselves lucky that they don't have to deal with this animal.

Pocket gophers are solitary animals, but large numbers can live in a relatively small area—sometimes as many as twenty animals share an acre (.4 ha). They breed in the spring and produce one litter of between three and six young each year. Pocket gophers are true vegetarians, eating roots, bulbs, tubers, annuals, perennials, shrubs, and trees. The animal's favorite food is alfalfa.

Pocket gophers thrive in loose-textured soil, pastures, and prairie lands. They spend most of their time below the ground, but will come up for short excursions. The gopher's strong front claws make digging easy.

The Damage They Do

Pocket gophers dig up lawns, forests, orchards, and gardens. The animals leave unsightly crescent-shaped mounds of dirt above their tunnels. One gopher can create as many as 200 mounds per year and one tunnel can extend over an entire acre (.4 ha). The holes and tunnels that they create can release water from dams and canals.

Wondering if you've got moles or gophers? Unlike the mole, gophers "plug" the entrance to their tunnel with dirt and vegetation. Gopher tunnels are usually deeper than mole tunnels, and they cannot be seen from above ground. Moles also tend to have volcano-shaped mounds while the gopher's is more fan shaped. Mounds and subsurface tunnels can damage mowing and haying equipment. The mounds are usually 12 to 18 inches (30.5 to 45.7 cm) wide and 4 to 6 inches (10.2 to 15.2 cm) high. Gophers usually build the tunnels that create these mounds in the spring and fall.

Winter snow makes it safe for gophers to take longer excursions above ground by providing them with cover should a predator appear. It is during the winter that gophers girdle and kill trees. Gophers leave tiny tooth marks that are sometimes confused with vole chewings. In the summer, gophers cause serious damage to alfalfa crops by eating roots, leaves, and stems. The animal also kills trees by eating the roots.

All rodents need to chew on things to keep their teeth sharp. Sometimes gophers damage underground wires and cables by chewing through them. In areas where gophers thrive, utility companies use hard, metal-jacketed cables.

Repellents

Some people claim that mothballs will discourage gophers, but I have not found this to be true. A wildlife biologist friend of mine has been able to repel gophers by shoving a cloth saturated with fox urine down the hole. He recommends freshening the rag about once a week for best results.

Thiram is another product that repels gophers. Spray or paint Thiram onto valuable plants to protect them. Unfortunately it, like all repellents, must be applied often.

It's possible to flood pocket gophers out of their tunnels with water. Just place a garden hose into the hole and fill it up. Ultrasonic devices and noisemakers do not appear to repel gophers. The gopher spurge plant, *Euphorbia lathyrus,* does repel gophers and moles. Be careful when handling this plant because it is poisonous and can irritate your skin and eyes. Plant gopher spurge as close to entrance holes as possible. If one plant is good, three are better!

Deterrents

Deterrents are the most effective means of preventing gophers from damaging plants. Installing a ½-inch (1.3-cm) galvanized hardware cloth fence around a plant or tree will keep gophers away. Push fencing underground so that it completely surrounds the roots of the plant you are protecting. It is much easier to install deterrents when starting a garden than when the garden is already established. To insure complete protection for your individual plants, hardware cloth is available in the form of a basket or bucket. Set the plant into the bucket, place the bucket into the ground, and fill the bucket with soil.

Control the weeds and you can effectively limit gopher damage. Eliminate the forbs, which have succulent large roots. This works especially well in orchards. By changing the soil conditions, you can discourage pocket gophers. Flooding the area or compacting the soil can encourage gophers to move elsewhere.

Protect underground cables and irrigation lines with either lead or PVC coating to prevent the animals from chewing on them.

Quick Tip

Installing a ½-inch (1.3-cm) galvanized hardware cloth fence around a plant or tree will keep gophers away.

The Victor trap can be an effective tool against pocket gophers.

Although these animals are usually underground, it is always a good idea to encourage gopher predators. Hawks, owls, bobcats, weasels, skunks, cats, foxes, badgers, and snakes all eat gophers. Raptor perches for hawks and owls work well. Putting out meat baits will attract predators such as foxes and coyotes. Laying black plastic tarps or wet burlap will encourage snakes to hang around.

Live Capture, Handling, and Relocation

It's difficult to catch pocket gophers in live traps. Since these animals live primarily underground, live trapping with Havahart-type traps isn't that practical. Gophers are not that hardy and if they are removed from their tunnel system, they will most likely die.

Lethal Methods

Trapping is the most practical method of reducing small to medium numbers of these rodents. Trapping is most effective in the spring before the young are born.

There is a box-type trap on the market for trapping gophers, but I don't recommend it because it is difficult to place in the hole and set properly. The commercial wire traps for gophers are specifically designed to fit inside their tunnels, disturb the soil the least, and are the easiest to use. Some commercial wire traps available to the public are the Death Clutch 1, Macabee, Victor, and the Guardian Gopher Trap. The #1 leg-hold foot trap ("jump trap") and the Conibear (110 or smaller) trap will also work.

No matter what trap you use, always stake it solidly above ground. Place two traps in each tunnel to increase your chances. Follow the entrance of the tunnel down into the ground until it splits. Put a trap in each tunnel so that you will catch the

Gopher-Free Gardening

Problems with gophers? The best way to keep gophers out of your garden is to create a raised bed prior to planting. Build a wood frame and tack hardware cloth to the bottom. Nestle this structure into the ground a little, add your dirt, and plant your garden. The hardware cloth will prevent the gopher from digging up to the plants. Protect individual plants by planting them in a hardware-cloth basket. The roots will still be able to grow through, but the gopher won't be able to eat the plant.

gopher coming from either direction. Once you've placed the traps, cover the hole with a piece of cardboard. This will keep out light and improve your chances for capturing the animal. If the animal detects any light, it will avoid the area. Gophers are solitary animals, each living in its own tunnel, so once you catch one, move on to another tunnel system.

There are grain-type poisons available for pocket gophers. Purchase acute toxicants and anticoagulants from most farm stores. Poisons must be fresh, as these animals will avoid eating anything that is moldy. Apply one or two teaspoons to each tunnel system. If you will be applying the poison to a number of tunnels, the Wilco Company makes an applicator called the Gopher Getter. Its probe, handle, and foot pedal make it easy to apply the material directly into the tunnel. The success of a poisoning campaign depends upon the applicator's ability to locate active burrows.

Fumigation techniques are not at all effective in gopher eradication. The animals either detect the odor or sense impending doom and quickly seal off the tunnel.

Best Baits

It's not necessary to bait a gopher trap. If you insist, lettuce and carrot tops are the best. One trapper swears by a peanut butter and molasses mix on whole-wheat bread.

Porcupines

The porcupine is a blackish-colored animal that is covered with more than 30,000 sharp quills. Also known as "quill pigs," these animals breed in the fall and have only one baby in the spring. The baby stays with the mother throughout the summer and the survival rate of the little one is usually quite high—if it stays off the road and away from motor vehicles.

Porcupines are mostly nocturnal and are active year-round. They are primarily vegetarians eating a variety of plants, garden crops, orchard fruits, twigs, leaves, and tree bark. Favorite trees include the ponderosa pine, aspen, willow, and cottonwood. Tooth marks are usually obvious on chewed trees.

There are only a handful of predators that are clever enough to attack the porcupine without getting a face full of quills. The coyote, bobcat, and bear are able to overcome the porcupine once and awhile, but it is the fisher that has the game figured out. It carefully rolls the porcupine over on its back and attacks from underneath where there are no quills.

It's easy to spot a porcupine, especially if there is some snow on the ground. Tracks leading to and from the cave or hollow tree will give the location away. Dens are usually littered with football-shaped droppings, which are about an inch (2.5 m) long. Often there are a number of chewed trees close to the den. Clipped twigs may be lying on top of the snow. During the winter, more than one porcupine may frequent the denning area. During the rest of the year the male lives a rather solitary existence. The year's young usually stay with the mother until she kicks them out of the den in the fall.

The Damage They Do

The porcupine is known for its ability to girdle trees. Porcupines usually strip younger trees at the base and girdle more

The porcupine is also known as the quill pig.

mature trees on the upper limbs. The animal loves to eat anything with salt in it. Reports of animals eating leather on horse saddles, harnesses, and belts are common. Damage to buildings and property (especially summer camps and homes) is a frequent complaint. Plywood and outhouse seats are all fair game to the porcupine. I have had boat trailer tires chewed on, and on one recent camping trip, a porcupine actually chewed through a friend's brake line on his vehicle. We were miles back in the woods and were lucky to have had a second vehicle.

Porcupines are not aggressive animals but they can be very persistent when they find something they want to eat. Their loud gnawing noises may wake you from a sound sleep. If you scare them away, they will often return in a short time.

Although porcupines are not aggressive, their quills are a major threat to any animal that tangles with them and can be fatal if not removed immediately. The quills are barbed and work deep into the victim. Should your pet have the misfortune of an encounter, snip the quill prior to pulling it out. The quills are hollow and if you just grab and pull, you actually make the quill expand. By snipping the quill, you relieve the pressure.

Repellents

Many of the taste-bad repellents effectively deter porcupines. Thiram sprayed or painted on trees, plants, or other material has been shown to keep porcupines at bay to some extent. Whatever the repellent, apply it often. A wood preservative called pentachlorophenol can work on plywood.

Deterrents

Fencing around small trees, shrubs, and gardens is the most practical method of protecting them from the porcupine. Guarding tree trunks with hardware cloth or aluminum flashing will keep porcupines from chewing the individual plants. Electrical fencing wire placed at the top of the normal garden fence will also deter them.

Quick Tip

Guarding tree trunks with hardware cloth or aluminum flashing will keep porcupines from chewing the individual plants.

Live Capture

If you wish to capture the animal alive and release it, I recommend the Havahart-type box trap. Select a trap that will hold a large porcupine. I prefer the one-door models to the two-door models. My favorite is the Havahart model 1079. If you have a two-door Havahart-type trap, fix it so that only one door operates. Lift the wire of the door that you would like to make inoperable away from the pan mechanism. Place the bait way under the inoperable door. When using the two-door traps, I also place a small block of wood or stone under the front part of the foot trigger. This forces the animal to go farther into the trap, making it is less likely that the front door will drop down on the porcupine's back and allow it to back out. Always stake down the two-door model so that the animal can't roll it over and get out. Bait the trap with salt tablets, placing most of the bait well behind the trigger mechanism. Porcupines aren't particularly smart and will easily enter a trap for the salt. When using this method, be warned that you may catch a skunk! Just carefully set the critter free and try again.

Lethal Methods

Porcupines are not protected by law so they can be trapped or shot year-round. I use a #2 leg-hold trap and anchor it firmly to the ground. When setting it in a den, hole, or log, make sure to set the trap off to one side or the other. People tend to place foot traps in the center of holes instead of where the animal's feet will actually fall. Unbaited killer traps such as the 220 Conibear can also be effective when set near porcupine denning areas. Do not use these traps if there is any chance of catching a domestic pet.

Some professionals use toxicants such as strychnine-laced salt blocks to kill porcupines. They place these blocks high in the trees or deep in the dens to prevent nontarget animals from getting into them. Purchase the blocks from the Animal Damage Control offices of the U.S. Fish and Wildlife Service. If hunting is legal in your area, it can sometimes be the simplest solution to the problem. Porcupines are not particularly wary and if you are somewhat quiet, you can easily approach them with a flashlight. In the wintertime it is easy to follow the animal's tracks through the snow. Porcupines can often be found sleeping on a tree limb, in the center of a hollow log, or in a rocky outcrop or cave.

Best Baits

The best bait for the porcupine is salt. Water softener tablets work great. Salt applied to a rag, sponge, or piece of wood will also do the trick. Baits such as apples and carrots can also work. Place the trap as close to the den or travel area as possible.

Handling and Relocation

In general, it is a bad idea to relocate porcupines because you will most likely be creating a problem for somebody else. Porcupines have a poor survival rate and chances are that you will relocate the animal to an area already saturated with porcupines.

Diseases

I am not aware of any porcupine diseases that threaten humans. If porcupine quills penetrate the skin of domestic stock or canines (particularly hunting dogs), they can be fatal if not removed immediately.

Rabbits

The rabbit is an abundant ground dwelling animal that spends its entire life within 3 acres (1.2 ha) of where it was born. Rabbits give birth to babies from April through September after a twenty-eight-day gestation period. Rabbits can have up to four litters each year with as many as five young per litter.

The Damage They Do

Rabbits damage gardens, shrubs, and fruit trees. Their love of carrots, tulips, and young apple trees has gotten many a rabbit in trouble. Rabbits are vegetarians and will quickly girdle the bark of a fruit or sumac tree.

Repellents

Rabbit repellents can be an effective but temporary solution to rabbit damage. Reapply repellents often. Blood meal and mothballs can work, but they will have to be reapplied after it rains. Garden stores have commercial products that also claim to work. Gardeners paint some repellents on their plant to make the leaves taste bad to the rabbit.

The cottontail rabbit

There are a variety of commercial repellents available to the consumer. All have some repelling qualities. Some of the more common ones are capsaicin, naphthalene, paradichlorobenzene, Thiram, tobacco dust, and Ziram.

Deterrents

A well-placed fence around the garden will keep most rabbits out. Although they are not good diggers, I recommend that you bury the fence a foot (.3 m) into the ground to prevent rabbits from digging under. Rabbits will try to squeeze through fencing, so make sure the mesh in the fence is small enough so that they can't get through.

Installing electric fencing around a garden is the most effective nontrapping technique available to the homeowner. Electric fences will also discourage woodchucks and raccoons. They are easy to set up and are available at most farm stores. Set one wire 4 inches (10.2 cm) and another wire 8 inches (20.3 cm) above the ground. Place colored flags at 6-foot (1.8-m) intervals. For some odd reason the flags have a repelling effect.

A more permanent solution to plant damage is to place hardware cloth or commercial tree wrap around the base of the trees or plants you would like to protect. Make sure to apply the wrap high enough to protect the tree in the event of deep snow.

Raptor perches can help discourage rabbit populations.

Quick Tip

Installing electric fencing around a garden is the most effective nontrapping technique available to the homeowner.

Hawks and owls like to perch on top of dead trees and poles to look for and pick off unsuspecting rabbits. You can encourage raptors by providing perches for them. Erecting long 4x4-inch (10.2x10.2-cm) poles into the ground around a garden will work. If you have an active falconry association in your area, you might be able to encourage one of their members to train their bird on your rabbits.

Changing the way you mow the grass around gardens can also help reduce rabbit populations. Cleaning out rabbit cover near the garden and creating wide, straight, grassy strips gives hawks and owls a better view of the rabbits.

Live Capture

If you wish to trap the animal yourself, I recommend a box or live trap. Foot traps are best left for the experienced nuisance wildlife agent. The best time to trap is during the winter when the food supply is low. Use a one-door box trap that is at least 9 inches (22.9 cm) wide and 18 inches (45.7 cm) long. Box traps built with solid walls work best. If you have the wire-type Havahart model, cover the trap to darken the inside.

Place the trap close to the hole, trail, or feeding area, with the entrance of the trap facing the hole or trail. Don't set the trap directly on the trail. Make a trail of bait leading into the trap, placing most of the bait well behind the foot pedal or trigger mechanism. This method lures the rabbit into the trap with a few free chunks of bait but not so much that the rabbit loses all interest in entering the trap. If you have a two-door

Rabbits use their razor-sharp teeth to bite off twigs cleanly.

Havahart trap, fix it so that only one door operates. Do this by lifting the wire that connects the door that you would like to make inoperable away from the pan mechanism. Place the bait way under the inoperable door. When I'm using a two-door trap, I also place a small block of wood or stone under the front part of the foot trigger. This forces the animal to go farther into the trap, making it is less likely that the front door will drop down on the rabbit's back and allow it to back out. Always stake a two-door model to the ground so that the animal can't roll the trap over and get out. Box traps work best if you sprinkle a few rabbit droppings inside. You may also be able to pick up rabbit scent spray from your local sporting goods store. Beaglers use the spray to train their rabbit-hunting pups.

Apply tree wrap high enough to prevent rabbit damage in deep snow.

Lethal Methods

Some people use sulfur or gas bombs to get rid of rabbits. Purchase gas bombs at most farm stores. Use gas bombs with caution because they can start fires under buildings or in dry grassy areas. I have found this method to be only moderately effective if used just after you see the animal go down the hole. To increase your likelihood of success, cover all but the entrance hole. Moisten the entrance hole, light the bomb, and place it into the hole. Cover the hole with earth and check back in a few days to see if the rabbit has redug the hole. Repeat the process if necessary.

Hunting can be also be effective. Check with the laws in your area to make sure it's legal before using this method. A hunter with a good beagle can seriously thin down the rabbit population. In the past, ferrets have been used to scare rabbits out of their holes. A special license is required to keep and use a ferret, however.

Trapping is also an option. For rabbits, set 110 Conibears (body gripping traps) in the holes. If you are using a foot trap, set it to the side of the hole, not in the middle. Setting the trap in the middle of the hole will only catch belly hair. Also use the stop-loss type with the extra spring, which puts the animal in a "half nelson" position. This will prevent it from breaking its leg and getting away. Check set foot traps often if you wish to release the animal. Rabbits are not very hardy and will expire

Quick Tip

Box traps work best if you sprinkle a few rabbit droppings inside. You may also be able to pick up rabbit scent spray from your local sporting goods store.

quickly if not discovered soon after capture. Therefore I consider foot traps a lethal method in this case.

Best Baits
Rabbits prefer fresh baits. A cut-up apple makes the best bait. Make a trail going into the trap, placing several apple chunks well behind the foot pedal. Rabbits also respond well to Brussels sprouts, carrots, cabbage, salt tablets, or lettuce. These baits are especially good for not attracting domestic pets.

Handling and Relocation

Rabbits are not particularly hardy when caught in a box trap. Therefore, if you intend to release it you should check the trap often and release the rabbit as soon as possible after it is caught. Rabbits can bite, but seldom do. In fact, you are more likely to get scratched by one than bit. Even so, never allow children to go near the trap. When handling a trapped animal, wear gloves and eye protection to prevent bites and infection. If you plan to release rabbits, they should be taken a mile (1.6 km) or so away from where you captured them. Most conservation departments have nuisance wildlife agents who can help relocate, remove, or dispose of the animal. Be sure not to release it where it will become a problem for someone else. If you are lucky enough to have a beagle club in your area, most will eagerly take any extra rabbits off of your hands. These clubs may even be willing to trap them for you. Beagle clubs use the rabbits for field trials. The beagles chase the rabbits, but do not catch or injure them in any way.

Diseases
Rabbits can contract tularemia, which is an infectious bacterial illness. It can be transmitted to humans by touch. Symptoms include fever, chills, nausea, headache, and cough.

Raccoons
The raccoon is a brownish-gray animal with a black, mask-like marking on its face and a series of rings on its tail. Raccoons can grow up to 40 inches (101.6 cm) in length and weigh as much as 35 pounds (15.9 kg). Raccoons mate in February and mothers give birth to two to four young in late April. Raccoons are most active at night, often paying a visit to the local

farmer's corn patch. Home can be a hollow tree, a hole in the ground, a vacant building, your fireplace chimney, or even a hayloft in a barn. Coons love to eat sweet corn, crayfish, strawberries, and grapes.

The Damage They Do

Raccoons are notorious for raiding a garden just when the sweet corn is ready for harvest. They are responsible for many dollars worth of damage to farmers' cornfields each year. Raccoons have the habit of climbing up the cornstalk and bending it over to the ground. They concentrate on small areas in the cornfield, usually close to the woods where they can escape for safety.

The raccoon is also known as the masked bandit.

A coon may enter a henhouse to either eat the eggs or the chickens. Raccoons carry away eggs before eating them and they generally bite the head off of chickens before eating them. Extreme mauling is usually the sign of an opossum, not a raccoon. Each year, the raccoon consumes many waterfowl eggs. For this reason, it's not uncommon to see flashing or predator guards on wood duck boxes.

This soffit is damaged from the weight of a raccoon.

Raccoons have also been known to damage buildings. I know of an instance where a raccoon pulled the Masonite siding off of a garage in order to get inside. The animal scratched out a 3-foot-wide (.9-m) hole. Raccoons living in buildings can cause other damage. The weight of the animals can often damage soffits and, if the animals are allowed to live there, urine stains will appear. Raccoons nest in trees, in old barns, and inside chimneys, often leaving behind piles of feces. These animals are extremely strong and they can get into just about anywhere they want to go.

Several years ago one newspaper reported that two raccoons had entered the home of a wheelchair-bound seventy-year-old woman. The animals got in through the woman's chimney, accidentally shutting the damper behind them. Before it was all over, the animals had destroyed her valuable Hummel collection and various other antiques, valued at more than $15,000.

Repellents

Repellents don't work very well for raccoons. I have seen one report suggesting that naphthalene or paradichlorobenzene may be somewhat effective in enclosed areas.

Deterrents

Installing an electric fence around a garden or henhouse can be an effective nontrapping technique to discourage the raccoon. Adding an electric wire 2 inches (5.1 cm) above your existing fence will do the trick. If you don't have an existing fence, place one wire at 4 inches (10.2 cm) above the ground and another wire at 8 inches (20.3 cm) above the ground. Electric fences are easy to set up and are available at farm stores. Around a garden, turn the fence on two weeks before your crop is ready.

Quick Tip

If you are experiencing problems with coons in your chimney, install a strong chimney guard or cap.

If you are experiencing problems with coons in your chimney, install a strong chimney guard or cap. There are several varieties available but only a few are strong enough to keep a coon out. Most are designed for squirrels and birds. Chapter 9 includes plans for a homemade cap that is sure to work.

Blasting an all-night rock and roll radio station in the center of the garden can be used as a temporary method to repel raccoons. Some people also use dogs to protect their crops. Most devices designed to frighten coons may work for a short time, but will not work in the long run. Raccoons are very smart and can quickly learn whether the danger is real or not.

Live Capture

Because raccoons are very strong and hard to hold, foot traps are best left for the experienced nuisance wildlife agent. To trap raccoons, I recommend the Havahart box trap. If you intend to use a box trap for raccoon, the one-door models are preferred. Whatever trap you use, make sure it is big enough for a large coon. My favorite is the Havahart model 1079. If you have a two-door Havahart trap, fix it so that only one door operates. To do this, bend the wire on the door that you would like to make inoperable away from the pan mechanism. Also place a small block of wood or stone under the front part of the foot trigger. This forces the animal to go farther into the trap to retrieve the bait, making it less likely that the front door will drop down on its back and allow it to back out. Always stake the trap to the ground so that the coon can't roll the trap over and escape.

To bait the trap, create a trail of bait leading into the trap, placing most of the bait well behind the trigger mechanism. Center the bait in the back of the trap so that the animal can't reach it through the side. The idea is to give the raccoon a few free chunks but not feed it a full-course dinner. Increase your chances by setting two or three traps. Don't be afraid to experiment with different baits.

Occasionally you will encounter a trap-shy raccoon. When this happens I use my secret weapon—the garbage can trap. The trap looks like an ordinary garbage can but once the coon gets in it, it won't be able to get out. I've provided instructions on how to build this trap in chapter 9.

Some raccoons will not enter the normal Havahart-type trap. When this happens, I turn to the garbage can trap. See my plans in chapter 9.

When a raccoon takes up residence in a chimney, try to trap it as close to the chimney as possible. If you place a trap on your roof, place a big enough piece of plywood underneath to prevent the trapped coon from ripping up your shingles. Getting raccoons out of a chimney requires considerably more work. I attach my Havahart trap to the top of the chimney flue with hardware cloth. Before affixing the trap, I insert a chimney brush all the way down the chimney and then use the brush to scare the coon up the chimney. If the coon is reluctant to come up, a sparkler shoved into the firebox will get it moving. Sometimes the coon will grab a hold of the brush and ride it up to the trap located at the top of the chimney. This system works best if you have a partner to help you; one of you can work the brush while the other lights a sparkler in the fireplace.

Foot traps can also be used to catch raccoons. Raccoons are very powerful, so anchor all traps tightly to the ground. When setting the foot trap, make sure that there is nothing nearby for the coon to grab onto. The coon is so powerful that it will pull itself right out of the trap. I use a #1½ coil spring trap. Make sure the traps are odor free and covered lightly with surrounding vegetation or dirt so the coon can't see them. Set the pan pressure to "hair trigger" by adjusting the screw underneath the pan. With the hair trigger setting, you will catch the coon on the center of the paw, reducing the chances of injury. If you plan to release the animal, use a strong noose or place it in a carrying cage for relocation. Always handle trapped animals with gloves and eye protection.

When domestic pets are a concern, I use rubber-jawed foot traps. Another option is to use a drag or grapple hook. Grapples are like giant fish hooks that move with the animal when it is caught. They usually tangle up on the nearest tree or bush. The advantage of the grapple hook is that it has more give than other hooks, and therefore can help reduce the possibility of injury.

Lethal Methods

It's easy to catch raccoons in body gripping traps such at the Conibear 220. Place these traps in holes, along runways, on

top of a chimney flue tile, or in confined areas using bait as an attractant. Make your own baited bucket set by cutting notches into the sides of a bucket to hold the springs and then place the bait in the back of the bucket. Only use this set where domestic pets will not be a problem, as it will not differentiate between a coon and your neighbor's cat or dog.

A well-trained coonhound is a valuable tool in controlling raccoon populations. An experienced dog will single out and remove the garden-raiding raccoon. Farmers will almost always welcome coon hunters on their land.

Aside from being wonderful companions, coon hounds are a great help when hunting for raccoons.

Best Baits

Raccoon prefer fresh baits to tainted baits. I have had great success with sweet corn. To make it even more appealing, I sometimes spread honey on the corn and scorch the whole thing with a blowtorch. Raccoons also love donuts, chocolate chip cookies, marshmallows, bananas, candy, and bread with honey on it. If catching cats is not a problem, try smoked fish, sardines, and cat food.

Handling and Relocation

It's also possible to hand capture young raccoons using a glove. The small ones will make a lot of noise but don't seem to know how to bite. Do not attempt to catch larger coons wearing a glove as they will be able to bite right through it! If you are dealing with a family of raccoons, capture the mother before grabbing the babies. A mother with babies is always easier to catch than the average raccoon, but be warned: She will be very protective of her young.

If you plan to release raccoons, take them at least 7 miles (11.3 km) away. Once you've caught a raccoon, you may want to contact your local conservation department. Most have nuisance wildlife agents who can help relocate, remove, or dispose of the animal. If the animal must be destroyed, shooting it with a .22-caliber rifle in the head is the most humane method.

After capturing a raccoon, disinfect the trap with a solution of half bleach and half water. And don't worry: A disinfected trap will not repel animals you wish to catch in the future.

Diseases

Raccoons can carry a variety of diseases including, rabies, distemper, and mange. Coons with rabies look wet around the face and eyes. I have not seen foam around the mouth as some cartoons suggest. A rabid animal looks thin and, in the later stages of the disease, it will drag its legs and lose control of its muscles. It will show no fear of people and it may be aggressive. A coon with distemper will look healthy, but will not be afraid of people and it may appear friendly. In the later stages of distemper animals experience high fever and may head for water to cool off before they die. Mange is actually a mite that burrows beneath the skin and causes the animal to lose the hair on the back of its head, body, and tail. Mange can also be fatal to the raccoon. Many raccoons carry a nematode in their intestine. If ingested by humans, these small worms can be fatal.

Rats and Mice

Rats and mice are rodents that are born hairless and with their eyes closed. The average rodent lives less than one year. They are gray and colorblind. Mice mate year-round and have five to ten litters per year, each time giving birth to about five young. Rats have six to twelve young per litter and females come into heat every five days. Breeding is also year-round, but slows down in the winter. Rats have about four to six litters per year and many produce more than twenty offspring per year.

The Damage They Do

Rats and mice are a common nuisance to many homeowners and are considered some of the most destructive animal pests in the United States. These animals raid bird feeders; eat and contaminate food supplies; create urine stains, odors, and noise in walls and ceilings; remove insulation from buildings; and cause flea infestations. These animals have also been known to nest in lawn mower and automobile engines, causing expensive repairs. Homeowners dealing with rats and mice should be most concerned about the rodent's ability to spread disease and its need to chew. They love to chew on wood and electrical wires, creating the dangerous possibility of fire. Girdling of ornamental shrubs and fruit trees can also be a problem.

Repellents

Some people say that mothballs placed around areas frequented by mice and rats will discourage them. I have not found this to

be true. In fact I have seen instances where mothballs were actually incorporated into a mouse nest! Ultrasonic devices can work for mice, but the effective area is limited to about one room. Ultrasonic devices do not seem to work on rats. Thiram and BioMet 12 are the best commercial repellents.

Mice and rats are not easily repelled by mothballs.

Deterrents

There are a variety of commercial products available to protect trees from rats and mice. I have found that common aluminum foil or hardware cloth works just as well. Make sure you wrap it loosely enough for the tree to grow and high enough to allow for deep snowfall.

Seal obvious entrance holes with screening or by filling the hole with expanding foam such as Great Stuff. Mice can squeeze through a ¼-inch-wide (.6-cm) hole. If you plug up an entrance, it is wise to set a trap near it to catch any critters that have been using it. Another way to keep rodents out of the house is to remove weeds and debris from around the structure. High grass and debris provide excellent hiding places and breeding grounds for these critters. Remove rat and mouse hideouts and predators may have a better crack at catching them.

Quick Tip

Another way to keep rodents out of the house is to remove weeds and debris from around the structure. High grass and debris provide excellent hiding places and breeding grounds for these critters.

Live Capture

If you do not wish to hurt or handle the rodent, use a Havahart-type box trap. There are several varieties on the market. Just make sure the trap is the right size for the critter you are after. Sprinkle a trail of bait that leads into the trap, placing most of the bait well behind the foot pedal or trigger mechanism. This draws the animal into the trap but doesn't fill up the mouse or rat before it steps inside. Some live trap models can catch more than one critter at a time. A caught mouse acts as an attractant to other mice, so leave it in the trap for a day or so.

Make a homemade trap from a 5-gallon (19-l) plastic bucket, a coat hanger, a soda can, and a board. Straighten the hanger and slide it through a hole punched in the bottom of the soda can until it emerges from the top. Smear some chunky peanut butter on the can and lay it across the top of the bucket. Prop a board against the bucket to create a ramp that the animal can climb up. When the rodent climbs up the ramp to try to get the peanut butter, it will fall in. Add several inches of water to the bucket to make this a lethal solution.

Lethal Methods

To remove rats and mice from the home try trapping, using poisons, placing glue boards, or purchasing an aggressive cat!

Trapping is a good solution because you don't use any hazardous poisons, you can see whether or not you've been successful, and the animals don't die in the walls and emit foul odors. The snap trap works best for rats and mice. These are the traps people rely on to catch rodents, but often they are not used to their maximum potential. Since rodents are shy creatures, they tend to hug walls and other structures. Set traps with the trigger as close to the wall as possible, not out in the middle of the room.

Hanging a trap so that the rat has to reach up to get the bait works best.

The best way to set a mousetrap is to hang it. By hanging the trap, you increase your chances of catching a rodent. Use fishing line to hang the trap on a side wall along which the critter has been known to travel. Hang it so that the bait pan is about 2 inches (5.1 cm) high for mice and 4 inches (10.2 cm) high for rats. The rat or mouse will lift its head up to investigate the bait and get snapped right across the neck. The fishing line will prevent the critter from dragging off your trap.

Even mousetraps set on the ground should be tied down to save time looking for the caught critter. Some commercial snap trap companies claim they have built "the better mousetrap."

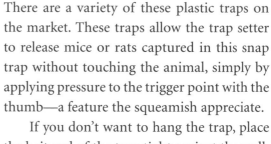

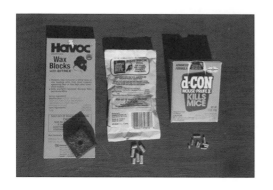

Poisons come in wax blocks or in pellets.

There are a variety of these plastic traps on the market. These traps allow the trap setter to release mice or rats captured in this snap trap without touching the animal, simply by applying pressure to the trigger point with the thumb—a feature the squeamish appreciate.

If you don't want to hang the trap, place the bait end of the trap tight against the wall. Setting two traps together always works better. Either set both traps side by side with the bait ends up against the wall or set the traps against the wall, end to end, with the bait ends on the outside.

Poisons can be very effective in controlling rodents, but this method does have its drawbacks. The animal can crawl off and die in your wall, creating an unpleasant odor. Or nontarget animals such as domestic pets may eat the poison. Prevent pets from coming in contact with the poison by making a bait station from which to dispense it. Use wood boxes, plastic piping, or drainpipes to make a bait station. A covered box with two holes approximately 2 inches (5.1 cm) in diameter to let in a rat will also work fine. This works best for the granulated d-CON poison.

This plastic pipe bait station keeps pets out but still lets rats and mice in. See chapter 9 for directions on how to build one.

For stick or wax baits, I use a 1-foot-long (.3-m) piece of drainage tile. I wire the poison to the top of the tile so the animal can't drag it out. See my instructions for building your own bait station in chapter 9. Place the stations along walls, in barns, and anywhere else rodents are a problem. When using a bait station, make sure to anchor it with a rock or some other heavy object, so that domestic animals won't tip it over and eat the bait. I have had very good luck with a product called Just One Bite. Apply the poison for seven to ten days, or until the rodents are no longer eating the food. Most poisons are anticoagulants. Of course, if you don't wish to make your own bait station, there are some commercial models available through your local farm or hardware store.

Another lethal solution is to shoot rats at night using a flashlight, a .22-caliber rifle, and birdshot. Make sure to observe local firearm restrictions. My method is to strap a small flashlight to the front of the barrel, adjusting the flashlight so that the shot pattern falls in the center of the light beam at a distance of about 20 feet (6.1 m) away. Focus the center of the beam on the rat and pull the trigger. It's a very fast solution to your nuisance animal problem.

Another method for catching rodents is a glue board. Some rats and mice become snap-trap shy, making these boards an effective alternative. The concept is simple. When the rodents walk across the sticky paper, they get stuck. Check the glue boards often, as a larger rat may chew itself free, depending on how securely it is stuck. You will find glue boards in most hardware stores. They are available in small and large sizes; use the small for mice and the large for rats.

Best Baits

My favorite bait for catching rats and mice is peanut butter mixed with birdseed. Place the bait on small chunks of bread or directly on the trip pan. Rodents also seem to like cheese, cereal, small nuts, oatmeal, sunflower seeds, and popcorn.

Handling and Relocation

Rats and mice can bite, so never allow children to go near a trap. To protect yourself from bites and infection when handling a trapped animal, wear gloves and eye protection.

Diseases

Rodents carry parasites that can transmit disease to humans. They are also known to carry salmonellosis (food poisoning), rickettsialpox, lymphocytic choriomeningitis, leptospirosis, rat bite fever, tapeworms, and ringworms. Plague is transmitted by the fleas that live on rats and other rodents.

Skunks

The skunk is a nocturnal animal known for its offensive odor and for the characteristic black-and-white stripe down the middle of its back. A skunk's body can grow as long as 15 inches (38.1 cm). Its tail is longer than its body, measuring about 17 inches (43.2 cm). Skunks mate in February or March and give birth to between two and sixteen young within fifty-six days. Skunks are not true hibernators, but they do go into a drowsy state during extremely cold weather. They generally live in old woodchuck burrows, but commonly seek shelter under buildings, woodpiles, and stone walls. When frightened, a skunk can spray objects up to 10 feet (3 m) away and is able to spray four times before running out of its odorous liquid. Contrary to popular belief, young skunks can spray. The rule is: If they can walk, they can spray! Adult males are more aggressive and are the most apt to spray.

The Damage They Do

Besides emitting a bad smell, skunks can cause a lot of damage to residential property. Skunks turn over the sod and dig small holes in the lawn while searching for grubs—a favorite food. Skunks can pinpoint the grub's location using their keen sense of smell. The holes they dig are usually 1 ½ inches (3.8 cm) wide by 3 inches (7.6 cm) deep. Every now and then a skunk will become particularly aggressive and really rip up the soil. Skunks not only dig for grubs; they are one of the few animals that will readily dig up a ground hornet's nest and eat the larva.

A skunk may enter a henhouse, but it usually will not kill the chickens. It will go for the eggs instead, eating them by opening one end and licking out the inside. Skunks will rip small holes in plastic garbage bags left out in the open, but they do not spread the garbage all over as raccoons would do. I once misinterpreted small holes in my garbage bags, thinking they were caused by rats. I set a foot trap and was very surprised when I caught a skunk. Removing a skunk from a foot trap is not easy!

If a skunk can walk, it can spray. Adult males are always more aggressive.

Skunks make holes like these when they are looking for grubs.

Repellents

Mothballs (naphthalene) can be scattered in the den area of a skunk to repel it. Liquid ammonia placed on a rag or in a pan can also work.

Deterrents

Grubicides kill the grubs skunks dig for, which makes your lawn less appealing to the skunks—no grubs, no skunks. Applying appropriate pesticides may help. I suggest you contact your local cooperative extension service for information on the most up-to-date product and its application.

Sometimes skunks that have taken to living under buildings can be jolted from an area with bright lights and loud rock and roll music.

Live Capture

If you wish to trap the animal, the one-door Havahart-type box trap works best. Foot traps should be left for the experienced nuisance wildlife agent. Select a trap that is big enough to hold a large skunk. Before setting the trap be sure to place a piece of plywood underneath, as the skunk will rip up the soil all around the trap trying to get out. Leave enough room around the trap to place a blanket over it once the animal is caught. Do not place a blanket over the trap prior to catching the animal because the skunk will pull the blanket into the trap and rip it up.

A skunk wrapped up in a blanket will not spray because it cannot see the threat.

Always place the trap as close to the skunk hole or the animal's travel area as possible. Bait the trap with tiny white marshmallows. Make a trail of bait leading into the trap, placing most of the bait well behind the foot pedal or trigger mechanism. Refer to chapter 5 for more information. If you have a two-door Havahart-type trap, fix it so only one door operates. To do this, lift the wire of the door that you would like to make inoperable away from the pan mechanism. Place the bait way under the inoperable door. With these two-door traps, I also place a small block of wood or stone under the front part of the foot trigger. This forces the animal to go farther into the trap, making it less likely that the front door will drop down on its back and allow it to back out. Always fasten a two-door model down so that the skunk can't roll it over and get out.

My favorite box trap is the Havahart model 1079 professional box trap. I modify these traps by adding a sheet metal roof and back to them. Once I catch a skunk, this solid metal blocks the skunk's view, so I can sneak up on it and lay a blanket over the top of the trap. I have found that a skunk will not spray in total darkness. The sheet metal and the blanket are the best way that I have found to cover the trap.

Handling and Relocation

If you use your head, handling a skunk in a box trap is not as intimidating as it seems. Cover the trapped skunk with a blanket, sheet, or tarp. To do this, very slowly and quietly approach the animal with tarp extended in front of you. If the skunk does spray, the tarp will protect you. If the skunk acts agitated, pats its feet, or turns its back to you, stop your approach and wait a moment until it settles down. Once you've covered the trap, tie the tarp securely around it. A covered skunk cannot see danger and will not spray. I have moved and relocated hundreds of skunks using this method and I have never been sprayed.

Several people have told me that if you quickly pick a skunk up by the tail, it can't spray you. The theory is that the skunk needs to dig its feet into something (like the ground) to put enough pressure on its scent sac to spray. *I* have never had the nerve to try this myself but others swear it works.

If you plan to release the skunk, take it at least 7 miles (11.3 km) away from where you captured it. The average home range of a skunk is about 1 mile (1.6 km), but many travel as far as 5 miles (8 km) during the mating season. Once you catch a skunk contact your local conservation department. Most offices have nuisance wildlife agents who can help relocate, remove, or dispose of the animal in such a way that the skunk will not spray. I release skunks by setting the covered trap under the driver's side door of my truck. Sitting in the truck, I open the window, lean out, and open the trap door by hand or with a string. From the safety of my vehicle, I carefully watch the skunk leave the trap.

Release skunks odorlessly from the safety of a vehicle. Use a string to raise the trap door.

If you do get sprayed, the best skunk deodorizer I have found is a material derived from orange peel extract. It is called Formula ni-712 and is produced by a company called Neutron Industries. When a skunk has sprayed and I want to reduce the odor, I saturate pieces of cardboard with this orange extract and place it anywhere the odor lurks—under porches, buildings, crawl spaces, or couches.

Lethal Methods

If you decide to euthanize the animal, shooting it in the head with a .22-caliber rifle is the most humane method, but be prepared for the odor. Drowning the skunk or gassing it is the most odor-free method available to the average homeowner.

The best, odor-free way to get rid of a skunk, is to watch it go down a hole and then use a smoke bomb or other fumigant. Block all secondary holes prior to lighting the bomb, making sure none of the fumes escape. Only use smoke bombs where fire is not a concern. Other lethal techniques are risky at best. Skunks are easy to catch in foot traps but hard to release once caught. Conibear bucket sets will easily catch a skunk, but be prepared for the spray. Avoid using this method when domestic pets are present.

Best Baits

Skunks prefer tainted baits over fresh baits, although I've had great success using tiny white marshmallows, which don't attract domestic pets. Other baits that seem to work well with skunks include chicken entrails, fish, sardines, cat food, peanut butter, mayonnaise, and bacon. Avoid using fish baits, cat food, and bacon if domestic pets are a concern.

Diseases

Skunks can carry diseases such as rabies, distemper, and mange. They are one of the most common carriers of rabies. A skunk that is aggressive and bites should be considered sick. Anyone bitten by a skunk should destroy it and have it tested for rabies. Do not ruin the head, as this is the part your health agency will be testing. Never allow children or pets near the trapped animal. To protect yourself when handling a skunk, wear gloves and eye protection.

.Skunks with rabies look wet around the face and eyes. I have never seen foam around the mouth like some cartoons suggest. A rabid animal looks thin. In the later stages of the disease, the animal will lose control of its muscles and drag its legs. It will show no fear of people and may be aggressive.

A skunk with distemper will look healthy, but won't be afraid of people and may appear friendly or stupid. In the later stages of distemper animals overheat and may head for water to cool off before they die. Mange is actually a mite that causes the animal to lose the hair on the back of its head, body, and tail. Mange can be fatal to the skunk.

Snakes

Snakes are usually categorized as either poisonous or nonpoisonous. A poisonous snake can be identified by its triangular

head, elliptical pupils, and pit between its eye and nose. A nonpoisonous snake has a narrow head, round pupils, and no pit. Some snakes are livebearers and some are egg layers. Common livebearers are the garter snake, water snake, copperhead snake, and rattlesnake. The black racer, king snake, rat snake, and hog nose snake are all egg layers. The common garter snake mates in the spring

The common garter snake can frighten people. It releases a foul odor when disturbed.

and can produce from twelve to seventy young by late summer. The adult garter snake grows to about 2 feet (.6 m) long and is about ¾ inch (1.9 cm) in diameter.

The Damage They Do

The fear of nonpoisonous snakes such as the garter is unfounded, but to many people, the sight of any snake is frightening. Nevertheless, even good snakes can overpopulate an area and create a nuisance by their presence and foul odor. Nonpoisonous snakes can also deliver a pretty good bite. Water snakes can bite very hard and leave tooth marks on your skin. Garter snakes will strike at you, but they don't have large enough teeth to do serious damage.

Every year, I remove approximately twenty-five garter snakes from one customer's property. Although the woman is not afraid of these snakes, she complains of the strong, foul odor the snakes produce when disturbed. They usually sun themselves by her back door or rest under her kitchen flooring. The odor permeates her whole kitchen.

Repellents

Repelling nuisance snakes can be tricky at best. Although there is a commercially produced snake repellent on the market called Snake Away, I have not had much success with the product. It smells like mothballs to me and has some serious warnings regarding its use around pets. There are no registered sprays, dusts, or poisons capable of repelling snakes.

Deterrents

Snakes can be controlled by removing their preferred type of habitat and food supply. Snakes love to live in stone walls and cracks in foundations. Seal cracks and other entry points with mortar, ¼-inch (.6-cm) hardware cloth, or expanding foam such as Great Stuff. Snakes also like woodpiles and other debris. Remove these habitats or move them away from the home if possible. A great number of snakes in one area generally suggests a large rodent or insect population. Start a mouse trapping or insecticide campaign to get rid of the food supply and the snakes will look for greener pastures.

Fencing can deter snakes. I use ¼-inch (.6-cm) hardware cloth. To fence off a playground area or child's sandbox, wrap the fencing around the area, burying the fencing 6 inches (15.2 cm) underground and slanting it outward at a 30-degree angle.

> **Quick Tip**
>
> *Snakes love to live in woodpiles, stone walls, cracks in the foundation, and other debris. Remove these habitats or move them away from the home if possible.*

Live Capture

Most nonpoisonous snakes can be hand captured with a noose or a forked stick, or simply by sweeping them into a bucket with a broom. Once I've pinned down or noosed the snake, I grab it by the head and place it in a burlap sack or a small garbage can. I always wear gloves.

Sometimes snakes can be easily spooked, which makes them hard to locate. Snakes like cool, damp, out-of-sight places to hide, and for some reason, they like to crawl under wet rags. I have found that placing a wet towel or burlap sack where the snake frequents can be successful. Place the wet towel or sack on the floor where you last saw the snake. Wait a couple of hours and then check it by approaching and lifting the rag quietly. If the snake is there, you have the option of capturing and relocating it or destroying it.

Lethal Methods

There are no known snake traps on the market, although glue boards designed to catch mice can work on smaller breeds of snakes. Attach several glue boards side by side on a large piece of plywood. Make sure the multiple boards are fastened down so you don't have to go looking for the snake. Place the plywood where the snake travels or suns itself regularly. Once the snake is stuck on the strips, you can dispatch the critter or release it by using cooking oil as a releasing agent.

Where firearms can legally be used, I have found that birdshot will quickly immobilize the largest of snakes. Shooting is the fastest and most effective way to get rid of snakes if the situation is conducive to it. Where firearms aren't allowed, many snakes are destroyed by the simple swing of a shovel or a club. Certain snakes are protected by law so check with your local fish and game department before killing one.

Best Baits

I know of no baits that are useful in catching snakes. Snakes eat insects, rodents, and frogs.

Handling and Relocation

I wear leather gloves when handling all snakes and release them at least 10 miles (16 km) from the capture site.

Snapping Turtles

Snapping turtles can grow up to 3 feet (.9 m) long, with females growing larger than males. In the early spring the female lays between twenty and thirty round eggs. The young hatch ninety days later. Turtles become dormant in colder areas, but many remain active year round in southern regions. Snapping turtles can live to be more than twenty-five years old. They eat a variety of plants and animals, including weeds, crayfish, carrion, insects, fish, and baby ducklings.

The Damage They Do

Turtles are known to eat both fish and baby ducklings; biting with lightning speed, turtles can be very dangerous to humans. Every summer at our lake in the Adirondacks, we watch as a mother mallard duck parades her eight or nine ducklings past our dock. By the end of the summer, that original group of eight or nine ducklings is reduced to one or two by the local predators—mostly snapping turtles. We have also found that we cannot leave a stringer of fish on the end of the dock overnight because by morning the snapping turtles will have eaten all of them.

Sometimes when I fish backwoods Adirondack ponds for brook trout, snapping turtles follow me around the pond, trying to eat the stringer of fish hanging over the side of the boat.

Repellents and Deterrents

There are no repellents available for snapping turtles. The only way to encourage a snapping turtle to leave a pond is to drain it. Extreme, but it works.

Live Capture

Turtles can be captured with a large, long-handled fishnet. I watch for moving weeds or the turtle's bubble trail to see what direction the turtle is heading, then make the grab.

A snapping turtle this size could deliver a nasty bite.

Another option is to catch the turtles while they are hibernating. Because a snapper can easily bite off your finger, only an experienced handler should attempt this technique, which is called "noodling." To noodle a turtle, use a long hook to poke around old muskrat holes, logs, and spring holes searching for hibernating snappers. A hibernating turtle offers little resistance.

There are several commercial turtle traps available to the consumer. They all work similar to a minnow trap. The hoop net design is the most common. Place smelly fish bait inside the trap. The turtle enters through a small funnel-like opening. Once inside, it can't figure out how to get out. Place these traps in shallow-enough water so that the turtle can get some air. The turtle will struggle much less if it can stick its nose above the water. Set traps in quiet areas of ponds and streams. Muddy bottom areas are better than rocky ones as the turtles can camouflage themselves better and there is generally more food available in these natural areas.

Make your own turtle trap by building a box frame and

covering it with fish netting and hardware cloth. For dimensions and other details about the trap, see chapter 9.

Lethal Methods

An easier way to catch snapping turtles is to attach a small fishhook (#6) to a floating bottle with about 5 feet (1.5 m) of twenty-pound fishing line. I bait up a bunch of these traps and drop them in likely locations such as backwashes, muddy bottom areas, and slow-moving areas of large streams. When a snapper takes the bait, the bottle starts moving. I simply grab the bottle and lift it slowly out of the water. The turtle won't resist until it nears the waiting net.

An empty bleach bottle makes a great bobber when trying to catch a snapper.

Shooting can work under the right circumstances. Be sure to check for local firearm restrictions before attempting this. Buckshot or deer slugs will stop a turtle quickly at close range. Aim for the head if you're using buckshot and for the shell if you're using a slug. Buckshot works best if the turtle is moving through the mud 6 inches (15.2 cm) or so underwater. If you cannot see the turtle, watch the direction of the turtle's breathing bubbles and aim about 1 foot (.3 m) in front of the lead bubble. If you are aiming for the shell, watch for ricochet.

Best Baits

Catfish heads and cut-up carp are the best baits for snappers. Bloody red meat, fish, and sardines are also effective.

Handling and Relocation

Handle snapping turtles with extreme caution as they can snap a broom handle in two with their powerful jaws. The best way to handle a snapper is to use a capture stick or noose (see chapter 6). Noosing the animal around the head is the safest way to grab it. It is possible to pick up a snapper by the tail, but be careful—this critter's neck is longer than you think and it could reach around and snap at you. Always wear gloves and hold the snappers out away from your body. If you intend to relocate the animal, you must take it to a completely different watershed.

Diseases

To my knowledge, snapping turtles carry no diseases that are harmful to humans.

Squirrels

Gray, red, and flying squirrels are the three most common species encountered by nuisance wildlife agents. Squirrels mate during the late winter and females give birth to between three and six young as early as March. The babies stay in the nest for ten to twelve weeks. Squirrels may have a second litter later in the season. Flying squirrels are strictly nocturnal and are more common than most people think. Red squirrels prefer to live in pine or spruce forests, while gray squirrels reside in hardwood forests and suburbia.

The Damage They Do

Squirrels raid bird feeders, fall down chimneys, and invade peoples' homes. Squirrels will readily take up residence in an attic if they can find a way into a house. They will quickly chew out a small hole on the corners of a fascia or soffit to gain access. Squirrels in an attic create many problems. The creature's urine smells and can stain the ceiling. If squirrels are not evicted immediately, parasites such as fleas can become a serious problem. Also, the sound of squirrels scratching on the ceilings can be very annoying. Squirrels love to chew on wood and electrical wires, creating the possibility of fire. One squirrel can do a lot of damage in a hurry if it is not discovered.

Young gray squirrels can be entertaining when they aren't raiding your bird feeder.

This red squirrel has chewed its way through wood shingles.

Repellents

Some people claim that mothballs will discourage squirrels. I have not found this to be true. I have actually seen a litter of squirrels with mothballs in their nest! A wildlife biologist friend of mine claims that he has been able to keep squirrels off of his bird feeder by hanging a cloth saturated with fox urine from it. For best results, he recommends freshening the rag about once a week. Look for fox urine in hunting stores; it is sold as a cover scent for bow hunters.

Thiram is a commercially produced repellent used to keep squirrels from chewing. Methyl nonyl ketone crystals can be sprinkled on the floor or in the attic to repel squirrels. Purchase these crystals from Market-Tech Industries (refer to the product manufacturer list on page 172 for contact information).

Deterrents

To prevent squirrels from climbing up your bird feeder, place flashing underneath it or hang a rag soaked in fox urine from it.

When the animals are out on their daily feeding forays, seal all entrance holes with screen, hardware cloth, or expanding foam sealants such as Great Stuff. Make sure that all squirrels are out before trying this technique, otherwise you could actually seal one inside, causing more problems. If you plug up an entrance, set a trap near the plugged hole to catch the critter when it returns.

Place flashing around trees to keep squirrels from climbing up them. This may sound extreme, but I recommend placing a band of flashing completely around the tree starting at about 2 feet (.6 m) above the ground. Place another band 6 feet (1.8 m) up. It is unsightly but it works! Also trim nearby tree limbs so that squirrels can't jump to the house.

If squirrels are finding their way down your chimney, spare yourself the shredded drapes and broken mementos and install a strong chimney cap. You'll find an excellent chimney cap design in chapter 9.

Live Capture

Trapping is the most efficient way to remove squirrels from attics and ceilings. When a squirrel gets inside your house, the quickest solution to this problem is to simply open the nearest door and let it out. Squirrels are usually not aggressive and will run from you. Sometimes a broom can assist the critter in making its exit.

Occasionally a squirrel will fall down the chimney and get stuck in the fireplace above the damper. When this happens, block the fireplace with the fireplace screen, glass window, or a piece of plywood. Before opening the damper, place several foot traps or some glue boards on the floor of the fireplace. Then open the damper and move away quietly. In a few minutes, the squirrel will crawl down into the main fireplace and get caught in the foot traps or glue boards. Simply noose the animal and release or destroy it.

If you wish to trap squirrels, I recommend the Havahart-type box trap for most situations. The one-door box traps work better than foot traps and are easier to use. Be sure the trap is big enough to hold a large squirrel. Make a trail of bait leading into the trap, placing most of the bait well behind the foot pedal or trigger mechanism. This attracts the squirrel to the trap, but doesn't give it too much bait. If you have a two-door Havahart trap, fix it so that only one door operates. Also place a small block of wood or stone under the front part of the foot trigger. This forces the animal to go farther into the trap, making it is less likely that the front door will drop down on its back and allow it to back out. Always stake the two-door model to the ground so that the squirrel can't roll it over and get out.

Use foot traps or glue boards to catch squirrels that fall down your chimney.

My favorite box trap for the gray squirrel is the Havahart model 1079. This trap might seem a little large for squirrels, but I have found that gray squirrels will enter a larger trap more readily than a smaller one. When trapping the red or flying squirrel, buy a medium-sized trap.

Lethal Methods

Use foot traps with caution around pets. These traps can be useful when there is not enough room between the ceilings and floorboards for a box trap. I spread peanut butter and birdseed directly on the pan of a large (#2) fox-type trap. Set the trap on "hair trigger" by adjusting the screw underneath the bait pan counterclockwise. The large trap will kill the squirrel almost instantly.

When a squirrel chews into the fascia or soffit of a building, I often place a Havahart or Conibear box right on the roof where the animal enters. Sometimes it takes a little maneuvering to level the trap. Always put a piece of plywood between the trap and the shingles to prevent the animal from ripping up the area underneath. Place model 110 Conibears on tree limbs to catch squirrels en route from the tree to the hole. Or, if the hole is large enough, place a 110 Conibear right inside the hole.

A Conibear box baited with walnuts will catch every squirrel that passes by.

Snap traps are not big enough for the gray squirrel but they can be effective for smaller squirrels. See chapter 6 on how to hang a snap trap for best results.

Best Baits

Peanut butter spread on small chunks of bread makes great squirrel bait. Also try using peanuts, cereals, grains, walnuts, sunflower seeds, and popcorn. Use apples to attract flying squirrels. For some strange reason, placing a red rubber ball in the trap also attracts flying squirrels.

Handling and Relocation

Squirrels can bite severely so never allow children to go near the trap. Wear gloves and eye protection when handling a trapped animal to protect yourself against bites and infection. If you plan to release a squirrel, take it at least 7 miles (11.3 km) away from where you captured it. Do not release any animal where it will become a nuisance for someone else.

Diseases

Squirrels carry several parasites, including ticks and fleas. As with any warm-blooded animal, a squirrel infected with the rabies virus can easily transmit it.

Voles (Field Mice)

Meadow voles, also called field mice, make their nests on the surface of the ground. Pine voles live in small openings and underground burrows. Meadow and pine voles are usually brown or gray, but may vary in color. They are active day and night, all year long. Voles usually stay in a home range of about ¼ acre (.1 ha) and breed year-round. They may have as many as five litters of one to eleven young each year. Baby voles are born twenty-one days after conception.

A meadow vole

The Damage They Do

Voles chew on the bark of trees and are found primarily in orchards and Christmas tree plantations. Vole damage is often confused with chewings from rabbits or deer. The animals may burrow many runways in grass and ruin nice lawns. Voles eat grasses during the summer months, but turn to bark in the fall and winter.

Repellents

I know of no commercial repellents or frightening devices that are very effective on voles. Some commercial companies sell repellents with Thiram or hot pepper (capsaicin), but these are usually short-term solutions at best. BioMet 12 may be moderately successful.

Deterrents

Hawks and owls can consume many voles. Encourage these raptors by creating perches. Leave some dead trees in the area you wish to protect or actually plant long 4x4-inch (10.2x10.2-cm) poles into the ground to provide a perch.

Habitat manipulation can help with voles. Mow broad areas very close to the ground around trees. Remove brush piles and create straight laneways in the grass and brush to give hawks and owls plenty of room to swoop down on voles.

Fox and coyote consume a considerable numbers of voles, too. Lure these animals to your property by placing meat baits around the yard. A mowed grassy area attracts canines because they know that hunting a freshly mowed field is easier than hunting in tall grass. Farmers commonly have the company of coyote and fox when they are haying their fields.

Protect trees and ornamental plants from vole damage by wrapping them with ¼-inch (.6-cm) hardware cloth, burlap treated with creasote, or other forms of tree wrap. Push the tree wrap at least 6 inches (15.2 cm) below the soil.

Live Capture

If you are only after a few voles, capture them in covered live traps.

Lethal Methods

Poisons such as zinc phosphide and commercially produced anticoagulants work on voles and are available to the homeowner. Zinc phosphide baits are produced in pellets and grain. This poison works in just one feeding and should be applied twice each year, in the late spring and fall. I have found that the rolled oats variety is more effective than the treated corn. For the meadow voles, broadcast the toxin. Place it in burrows for pine voles. Be warned that this toxin may be hazardous to songbirds. Read the instructions thoroughly before using.

Snap traps work for voles. Place unbaited traps in the runways and cover them with cardboard.

During the winter, voles chew on pine and apple trees, and ornamental plants.

Place unbaited snap traps in vole runways, positioning the trap so that the vole walks on the trigger. Cover the trap with a cardboard box to increase your chances of success.

Best Baits

To catch voles in a live trap or a snap trap, I have found peanut butter, apple slices, corn, and commercial rabbit pellets work the best.

Handling and Relocation

Voles are not usually handled or relocated. If using a live trap, release voles at least ½ mile (1.3 km) away.

Diseases

Voles are not major disease carriers, but cases of plague, tularemia, and Lyme disease have all been recorded. Lyme disease is spread by ticks that attach themselves to these rodents.

Woodchucks (Groundhogs)

The woodchuck

The woodchuck or groundhog is a ground-dwelling rodent with a plump body and short legs. Woodchucks are brown, grow up to 26 inches (66 cm) long, and have a 6-inch (15.2-cm) brownish-black tail. They can weigh as much as 14 pounds (6.4 kg). Woodchucks are true hibernators and mating occurs in the spring. After a gestation period of thirty-one days, woodchucks have four to five young.

The Damage They Do

Woodchucks damage gardens, lawns, and hay lots. Their insatiable appetite for green crops and their ability to dig many, many holes are two things that get these critters into trouble. Woodchucks are vegetarians and like nothing better than to eat a fresh row of green beans, peas, or melon shoots. Woodchucks are not protected by fish and game laws.

Repellents

There are no known commercial repellents, but one writer reports that bobcat urine may work—finding the bobcat urine is the challenge! I once stuffed a gasoline-soaked rag down a woodchuck hole to encourage the critter to seek a new residence. The woodchuck never dislodged the rag from the hole, but I honestly don't know if I repelled that animal or killed it. I later learned that the gases from the rag might have asphyxiated the animal. Never use chemicals such as gasoline near water supplies and wells. Placing a garden hose down the hole and filling it with water can discourage woodchucks. You might have to try this a couple of times, but the chuck will eventually get the idea to go somewhere else.

Deterrents

Fencing the garden will slow a chuck down but be warned: They are excellent climbers. The fence must be at least 4 feet (1.2 m) high and buried 1 foot (.3 m) into the ground to prevent the woodchuck from digging under it. Installing an electric fence around the garden is the most effective nontrapping technique to discourage the woodchuck. Electric fences are easy to set up and can be purchased from most farm stores. Set two wires around the perimeter of the garden fence, one at 4 inches (10.2 cm) above the ground and the other at 8 inches (20.3 cm). For some strange reason, adding colored flags to a fence at 6-foot (1.8-cm) intervals deters some woodchucks.

A woodchuck nibbled the ends off these melon shoots before they could produce fruit.

Live Capture

To trap a woodchuck, use the Havahart-type box trap. Foot traps are best left for the experienced nuisance wildlife agent. One-door box traps work best. Make sure the trap is big enough to hold a large woodchuck and place the trap as close to the hole or trail as possible without actually setting the trap on the trail. Turn the trap so the entrance faces the hole or trail. Make a trail of bait leading into the trap, placing most of the bait well behind the foot pedal or trigger mechanism. Bananas are the best bait for woodchucks.

After a woodchuck dug these holes in the patio, I caught the little devil in a Havahart trap.

If you have a two-door Havahart-type trap, fix it so that only one door operates. To do this, lift the wire of the door that you would like to make inoperable away from the pan mechanism. Place the bait way under the inoperable door. Also place a small block of wood or stone under the front part of the foot trigger. This forces the animal to go farther into the trap, making it is less likely that the front door will drop down on its back and allow it to back out. Always stake a two-door model down so that the woodchuck can't roll it over and get out. My favorite box trap is the Havahart model 1079. Keep in mind that woodchucks may be reluctant to enter a trap that has held a coon, opossum, or skunk. Clean traps will always catch more animals then dirty ones.

Lethal Methods

Some people use fumigants, also known as sulfur or gas bombs, to get rid of woodchucks. I have found this method to be only moderately effective. They work best when used just after you see the animal go down the hole. To be most effective, cover all other holes and moisten the entrance to the hole where you will light the bomb. Light the bomb, toss it into the hole, and cover the hole with earth. Check back in a few days to see if the woodchuck has dug its way out of the hole. Repeat the process if necessary. You can purchase gas bombs from most farm stores for about $1 each. See chapter 6 for more information on using fumigants.

Body gripping or Conibear traps set in a woodchuck hole will take every woodchuck that goes in or out of the hole. I have found that it may take a day or so for a frightened animal to get caught. If there is a chance of catching domestic pets, use extreme caution with these traps. If this is the case, I wait until I see the chuck go down the hole. Then I set the trap and place a large box over the whole thing. Anchor the box so that it can't be easily moved and won't stop the working action of the trap.

Although hunting woodchucks is an effective way to eliminate them, there are fewer and fewer places where firing a gun is legal. If you are considering shooting an animal, check with your local fish and game laws first. In New York State it is illegal to discharge a firearm within 500 feet (152.4 m) of a building. If shooting is an option, a well-sighted rifle can quickly dispatch a woodchuck. I use a .222-caliber rifle with a bullet capable of reaching 250 yards (228.6 m). The common .22-caliber rifle is a poor choice because the bullets have a greater chance of ricocheting. I use the higher-speed .222-caliber 50 grain sx bullets that disintegrate upon hitting an object.

Best Baits

Woodchucks prefer fresh baits to tainted baits. Bananas are the best bait. To bait the trap, peel a banana and slice it as you would to put it on your cereal. Make a trail into the trap, placing several chunks well behind the foot pedal. Woodchucks also favor apples, string beans, lettuce, and peas. These baits are especially good for not attracting domestic pets.

I learned of the woodchuck's taste for bananas from one of my customers. The homeowners had a family of chucks that they enjoyed watching from their back deck. The mother wood-chuck had four little ones and as they grew, they became more and more of a nuisance, eating everything in sight. The woman called and asked me to catch the mother and little ones. We agreed that I would catch and release them together, unharmed, at a local nature preserve. I set the live traps and began to bait the trap with apple slices. When the woman saw this, she told me that they really preferred bananas. She had been hand-feed-ing them from her deck and had trained them to stand up and beg for the treats. She gave me a banana, I set the traps, and by the time I got home, the phone was ringing. I had caught all five woodchucks in less than an hour. Two small ones were in one trap! After that, I experimented at a commercial site that had a bad woodchuck problem. I caught more than thirty woodchucks that year in live traps baited with bananas.

Handling and Relocation
Trapped woodchucks will whistle and chatter their teeth as you approach—mostly for show. They can bite but seldom do. Even so, never allow children to go near the trap. When handling a trapped animal, always wear gloves and eye protection to pre-vent bites and infection. If you plan to release woodchucks, take them at least 5 miles (8 km) away from where you cap-tured them. Do not to release the animal where it will become a problem for someone else. Once you capture a woodchuck, it is better to call your local conservation department. Most will have nuisance wildlife agents who can help relocate, re-move, or dispose of the animal. When woodchucks are trapped out of an area, it doesn't take long for new ones to move in. Therefore, it's a good idea to check on the holes to see if any new animals have taken up residence. If the animal must be destroyed, the most humane method is to shoot it in the head.

To release a woodchuck without getting bitten, place the trap under the truck, lean out the window, and open the door from above.

Diseases
Woodchucks can carry rabies, distemper, and mange. Wood-chucks with rabies look wet around the face and eyes. I have

not seen foam around the mouth as some cartoons suggest. A rabid animal looks thin. In the later stages of the disease, the animal will lose muscle control and drag its legs. It will show no fear of people and may be aggressive. A chuck with distemper will look healthy, but it will be fearless and may seem friendly or stupid. In the later stages of distemper, animals overheat and may head for water to cool off before they die. Mange is actually a mite that causes the animal to lose the hair on the back of its head, body, and tail. It can also be fatal to woodchucks.

Woodpeckers

Although there are more than twenty-two species of woodpeckers, only seven of these species regularly cause problems for humans. Some of the more common troublemakers are the sapsucker, pileated, downy, hairy, red-bellied, flicker, and red-headed woodpeckers.

Most woodpeckers eat tree-boring insects, sap, seeds, berries, and nuts. The sapsucker is most noted for its ability to drill into fruit and nut trees. With its strong pointed beak, it

Woodpeckers are fond of suet.

can easily chisel out chips of wood. Its long tongue allows it to remove insects and sap from deep within the wood. The sapsucker and flicker are migratory birds, while all of the other species remain in the same habitat during the winter.

Woodpeckers have a different toe arrangement than most other birds. They have two toes that extend forward and two toes that extend backwards. This gives them more stability when clinging onto and drilling into trees. The birds build nests in trees, telephone poles, fence posts, orchards, and buildings. Most woodpeckers have four young each year and breed in the spring, between mid April and early May. The incubation period is twelve days and both sexes take turns keeping the white eggs warm.

The Damage They Do

Most complaints about woodpeckers involve the noise (drumming) they make or the damage they cause to trees. Noises are usually related to mating behavior, although the sound of one hammering away on the siding outside your bedroom window can be extremely disturbing. Woodpeckers drum on trees, the outside of buildings, metal pipes, flashing, siding, and even glass windows. The good news is that since this is a mating behavior, the drumming noises only last the length of the mating season.

Woodpeckers drill holes in search of wood-boring insects and tree sap. Many times the birds drill holes to allow sap to form, which in turn attracts the insects they like to eat. Woodpeckers also drill holes for nesting. Damage to buildings usually involves a series of holes in siding, shingles, or under the eaves. Some birds make a series of small holes, while other species create several large holes. Wounds are usually superficial and indicate an existing insect problem. Woodpeckers are more likely to attack softwoods than hardwoods.

Woodpeckers are colorful birds that are protected by federal law. Before taking any lethal action, contact your local U.S. Fish and Wildlife Service. On some occasions, they will issue special permits to remove particularly destructive woodpeckers.

Repellents

Repellents and deterrents work best when several methods are used together. Birds quickly catch on to these tactics, therefore I recommend rotating different repelling methods. Repellents such as scarecrows, helium-filled balloons with eyes, windmills, shiny pie tins, plastic owls, plastic snakes, and kites are all somewhat effective. Strips of shiny aluminum cut in 2-foot-long (.6-m) sections, 2 to 3 inches (5.1 to 7.6 cm) wide, can be thumbtacked to siding to keep birds away. Rock and roll music and electronically recorded bird distress calls also have some repelling effect. Purchase tape recordings of bird distress calls from the Johnny Stewart Game Calls Company (refer to the product manufacturer list on page 172 for contact information). If neighbors don't object, explosive devices such as bird bangers and propane cannons will scare woodpeckers.

Tactile repellents such as Tanglefoot, Roost-No-More, and Bird Stop can all be applied to the damaged area. Often, once the bird gets its feet stuck in the goo it decides to go elsewhere. These tactile repellents may change the color of your siding, therefore I recommend that you try a test strip in an unseen area prior to applying it to the damaged area.

Quick Tip

Woodpeckers are colorful birds that are protected by federal law. Before taking any lethal action, contact your local U.S. Fish and Wildlife Service. On some occasions, they will issue special permits to remove particularly destructive woodpeckers.

Deterrents

Blocking the bird's access to the damaged area can be effective. Exclusion with netting may be unsightly, but it is very successful. Hang the netting in front of the damaged siding. Netting with ½-inch (1.3-cm) mesh, available in most farm and garden stores, works well.

Getting rid of the food source is the best way to deter woodpeckers. Because insects are the bird's staple food, declaring an all-out war against bugs could solve your woodpecker problem. Since insects enter any available hole in siding, caulk all edges of siding (especially new siding). Since you are removing one food source, it might be wise to give the birds another option. Woodpeckers are extremely fond of suet. Installing feeders filled with suet a considerable distance from the problem area is an effective deterrent. If the woodpecker's drumming is the problem, removing the piece of metal, flashing, or loose siding may be the only solution.

Live Capture, Handling, and Relocation

Live capture and relocation of woodpeckers is not practical and is probably illegal in your state. The birds are not particularly hardy and would not survive relocation.

Lethal Methods

It is illegal to kill woodpeckers unless you obtain special permission from the U.S. Fish and Wildlife Service.

9

Plans and Designs

Making your own critter control traps and equipment can be fun, save you money, and, in some cases, provide you with a product that can't be purchased anywhere else, such as the garbage can trap. In this chapter you'll find detailed instructions on how to build my two favorite traps. The garbage can trap is guaranteed to catch that trap-shy raccoon that is causing you trouble. Solve snapping turtle problems with my snapping turtle trap—it will catch them every time.

In addition to the trap instructions, I've included plans for a chimney cap and a bait station. These creations will help you deter animals and keep domestic animals safe. Keep in mind that these gadgets are only as good and as safe as you make them. If you do not anchor the bait stations to the ground, for example, you run the risk of having a cat or dog knock the station around and possibly spill and eat some of the poison. If you use the materials I've suggested and carefully follow my instructions, the end result will be a safe product that serves its purpose well.

The garbage can trap—my secret weapon for a trap-shy raccoon.

The Garbage Can Trap

I designed my garbage can trap to catch the trap-shy raccoon that continues to raid your garbage, despite your efforts to trap the critter. Trap-shy coons usually have been captured in a live trap once or twice before. In my experience, these wise raccoons will avoid the average live trap, but dive right into this one, thinking it is just another garbage can. The garbage can trap is unlike any commercial trap on the market.

This trap works best when placed near other garbage cans or where the garbage is normally stored. Place it near a post, wall, or telephone pole, so that the raccoon can climb up the pole and drop down into the trap with ease. Tie the handles of the garbage can to the pole to prevent the coon from tipping the can over. Bait the trap with sweet corn, cat food, donuts, or sardines. Sweet corn is by far the best bait.

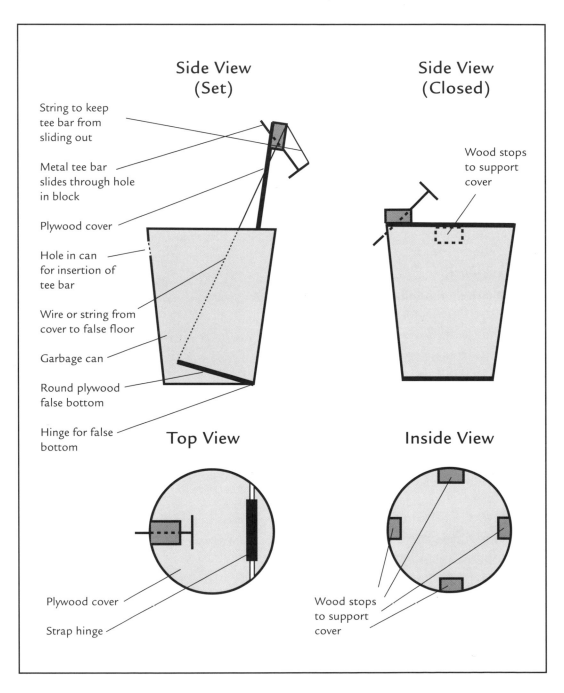

Side View
(Set)

Side View
(Closed)

String to keep
tee bar from
sliding out

Metal tee bar
slides through hole
in block

Plywood cover

Hole in can
for insertion of
tee bar

Wire or string from
cover to false floor

Garbage can

Round plywood
false bottom

Hinge for false
bottom

Wood stops
to support
cover

Top View

Inside View

Plywood cover

Strap hinge

Wood stops
to support
cover

Once you've caught and released the animal, it's easy to clean feces, urine, and stinky bait from the trap. I drill several small holes in the bottom of the can and just rinse it with a garden hose. Always disinfect the trap with a mixture of 1 part bleach to 3 parts water. A small spray bottle makes disinfection easy.

You will need:
1 metal garbage can, approximately 35-gallon (133-l) size
½-inch-thick (1.3-cm) plywood, enough to cut two circles to
    fit the top and bottom of the can
1 piece tee bar, 8 inches (20.3 cm) long
1 piece 2x4-inch (5.1x10.2-cm) wood, at least 20 inches
    (50.8 cm) long
1 strap hinge, 12 inches (30.5 cm) or longer
4 feet (1.2 m) of flexible wire or string
1 box 2½-inch (6.35-cm) drywall screws

Tools
drill and bits
sabre saw
screwdriver
tape measure
pencil

1.   Drill a hole in the can's side, 1 inch (2.5 cm) up from the bottom. Drill another hole in the bottom of the can, in line with the first hole.

2.   Drill several additional holes in the bottom of the garbage can for easy cleanup with a garden hose later on.

3.   Measure the diameter of the inside bottom of the garbage can. Subtract 1 inch (2.5 cm) from this measurement and cut the ½-inch-thick (1.3-cm) plywood in a circle to this diameter.

4.   Use a ¼-inch (.6-cm) drill bit to drill 2 holes directly across from each other on one side of the plywood circle. Holes should be about 1 inch (2.5 cm) in from each edge. One of these holes will be used to create a hinge, while the other will be used to connect the cover.

5.   Thread wire or string through 1 of these holes and then through the 2 holes you drilled in the side and bottom of the garbage can to make a hinge.

6.   Cut the 2x4-inch wood into 5 pieces, each 4 inches (10.2 cm) long. Screw 4 of these blocks of wood to the inside lip of the garbage can. Position the stops 1½ inches (3.8 cm) down from the top of the can, and place them around the inside edge as if on the face of a clock—one at 12 o'clock, one at 3 o'clock, one at 6 o'clock, and one at 9 o'clock (see diagram).

7.   With the stops in place, measure the diameter of the top inside lip of the can. Cut the remaining plywood into a circle just slightly less than this measurement. You want the cover to be loose enough to drop into the can freely, but not so loose that the coon can get its paws between the can and lid to pry it open.

8.   Measure 3 inches (7.6 cm) in from the edge of one side of the plywood cover and mark that spot with a pencil. Draw a straight line from one edge of the circle to the other through this point. Cut along the line with the sabre saw to create two pieces (see diagram).

9.   Now screw the strap hinge in place to reconnect the two pieces.

10.   To make the locking mechanism, take the remaining 2x4-inch (5.1x10.2-cm) block of wood and drill a hole slightly larger than the diameter of your tee bar. Drill the hole diagonally from one corner of the block to the other.

11.   Screw the block to the top of the plywood can cover, on the side opposite the strap hinge. Make sure that one of the holes that you just drilled into the block faces the strap hinge. Slide the tee bar through the drilled hole in the block.

12.   Close the cover over the can and use a pencil to mark where the tee bar touches the side of the garbage can. Lift the cover and drill a hole in that marked spot that is slightly bigger than the tee bar's diameter.

13.   Tie a piece of string to the tee bar to keep it from falling out when the trap is set. Thumbtack the other end of the string to the block of wood.

14.   Thread a piece of wire through the second hole in the can's false bottom (not the hole used to create the hinge), bring it over the edge of the plywood, and tie it off. Run this wire to the bottom of the plywood lid, and screw it to the underside of the plywood, about 1 inch (2.5 cm) below the lock block mechanism. When the lid is up, the wire should be taut, lifting the plywood bottom up at a slight angle. The plywood bottom should lift up just enough so that when the coon steps on it, the animal's weight will pull the cover down.

15.   Place bait such as sweet corn anywhere on the bottom piece of plywood.

Snapping Turtle Trap

With this trap, you can capture turtles in ponds, lakes, and slow-moving streams. Areas with muddy bottoms work best. Simply bait the trap with catfish heads, pieces of carp, bloody red meat, or canned sardines, then stake the trap to the pond, lake, or stream bottom. This turtle trap works similarly to the way a minnow funnel trap works. The turtle crawls into the trap through a funnel made of fishnet, which collapses behind the turtle, leaving it no way to get out.

You will need:

1 large piece of hardware cloth, 4 feet (1.2 m) wide and 10 feet (3 m) long

1 piece of hardware cloth, 31 inches (78.7 cm) square

1 piece of fish netting, 37 inches x 40 inches (94 cm x 101.6 cm)

20 garbage bag twist ties or light-gauge wire

10-inch (25.4-cm) metal or plastic stake

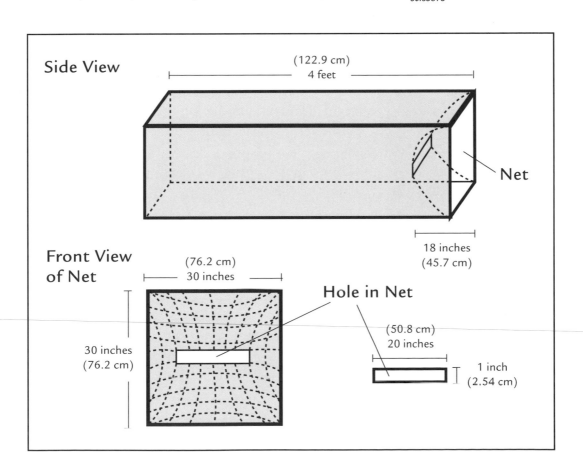

Side View

(122.9 cm)
4 feet

Net

18 inches
(45.7 cm)

Front View of Net

(76.2 cm)
30 inches

Hole in Net

30 inches
(76.2 cm)

(50.8 cm)
20 inches

1 inch
(2.54 cm)

1. Bend the 4x10-foot (1.2x3-m) piece of hardware cloth into the shape of a 4-foot-long (1.2-m) box with 30-inch-square (76.2-cm) openings on each end. To do this, place the hardware cloth on the ground in front of you. Measure 30 inches (76.2 cm) down along the cloth's 10-foot side. Use a needle-nose pliers to bend the entire 4-foot width of the cloth into a 90-degree angle.

2. From this bend, measure 30 inches again and bend the cloth into another 90-degree angle. Repeat this step until you've created a box. Use the needle-nose pliers to wind the loose wire ends of the last side into the ends of the first side.

3. Cover one end of the box with the 31-inch (78.7-cm) square of hardware cloth. Use the needle-nose pliers to bend and wrap the ends of the square into the wire ends of the box.

4. To create the funnel, use twist ties or light gauge wire to attach the ends of the fish netting to the open end of the box. The netting should form a bag inside the box.

5. Pull the netting bag out of the box. In the bag's "bottom," use a scissors to cut a slit 20 inches (50.8 cm) wide and 1 inch (2.5 cm) high. Push the net back into the box.

6. On each side of the slit you just cut, attach a piece of string. Use string to secure the funnel to the sides of the trap.

7. Place the catfish heads, pieces of carp, bloody red meat, or sardines in the center of the box.

8. Use the stake to anchor the trap to the pond, lake, or stream bottom.

9. Release captured turtles by cutting open the netting.

Homemade Chimney Cap

Unlike most commercial traps that only keep out birds and squirrels, this design will keep out bats and raccoons as well. The tight weave of the mesh allows smoke to escape from the flue but still prevents tiny birds from getting in, and very few of the chimney cap designs I have found will keep out bats. The strapping is strong enough to deter the most powerful raccoon.

Chimney cap

You will need:

½-inch (1.3-cm) mesh hardware cloth, large enough to overlap the flue you will be covering by 3 inches (7.6 cm) on each side

pipe strapping, long enough to circle the flue plus 4 inches (10.2 cm) for the bolt connection

1 bolt and nut, ¼ inch x 3 inches (7.6 cm x .6 cm)

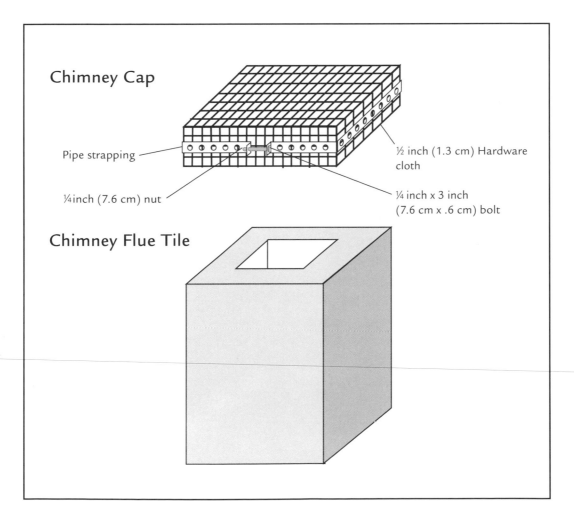

Chimney Cap

Pipe strapping

¼ inch (7.6 cm) nut

½ inch (1.3 cm) Hardware cloth

¼ inch x 3 inch (7.6 cm x .6 cm) bolt

Chimney Flue Tile

1.   Measure outside length and width of the flue tile. Add 6 inches (15.2 cm) to the length and width so there will be a 3-inch (7.6-cm) overlap along each edge of the chimney cap. Cut the hardware cloth to this measurement. For example, if the flue is 9 inches x 12 inches (22.9 cm x 30.5 cm), cut the cloth to measure 15 inches x 18 inches (38.1 cm x 45.7 cm).

2.   Using wire cutters, start from each corner of the cloth and cut a 3-inch-long (7.6-cm) diagonal line toward the center. These cuts will make it easier to bend the cloth around the flue.

3.   Place the hardware cloth over the flue and bend the corners down around the structure to create a lid.

4.   Place the pipe strapping over the top of the hardware cloth so that it encircles the outside of the flue. Pull tight.

5.   Slide the bolt and nut through the strapping and tighten with a screwdriver and crescent wrench.

Bait Stations
(For Poisons or Foot Traps)

Bait stations are most useful when you wish to get rid of nuisance critters such as rats, mice, weasels, and ground squirrels, but want to prevent domestic animals from getting into the bait. Use these bait stations to enclose poisons or foot traps. Poison drainpipe bait stations work well in chicken coops where rats and mice are attracted to the chicken feed. A bait station keeps the poultry from eating the poison but allows the target rodents in to feed. Our beagle club uses bait stations to get rid of weasels. The weasels kill the rabbits, which we desperately need for field trials. For weasels, we bait the wood box bait station with bloody meat or chicken heads and place a foot trap inside the box, just underneath the entrance hole. Always place bait stations as close to the feeding locations as possible and secure them with a rock or heavy weight to prevent domestic animals from tipping them over and spilling out the poison. I've provided two baiting options for the drainpipe station.

Poison bait station

For a plastic drainpipe bait station using wax bait, you will need:

1 section of drainpipe, 4½ inches (11.4 cm) in diameter and
    2 feet (.6 m) long
1 piece of wire, about 6 inches (15.2 cm) long
1 stick of Just One Bite wax bait
duct tape

1. In the middle of the drainpipe, drill 2 holes about 1 inch (2.5 cm) apart.
2. Thread the wire down into the pipe through one of the drilled holes and up out through the other drilled hole, leaving a large enough loop of wire inside the pipe to hold the bait stick.
3. Slide the bait stick into the pipe and through the loop. Pull up on the wire ends outside the pipe so that the bait is tight against the side of the pipe. Twist the ends of the wire together to hold the bait in place.
4. Use duct tape to cover half of the bait-station ends, as shown in the diagram.

5. Place the bait station in an area where you've seen the target animal. Use rocks to prop the station in an upright position to prevent domestic animals from getting to the poison.

For a plastic drainpipe bait station using grain bait, you will need:

1 section of drainpipe, 4½ inches (11.4 cm) in diameter and 2 feet (.6m) long

d-CON or other grain type bait, purchased in a ready-to-go bait box

duct tape

1. Place the ready-to-go bait box in the center of the pipe. Secure it to the bottom with duct tape.
2. Use duct tape to cover half of the bait-station ends, as shown in the diagram.
3. Place the station in an area where you've seen the target animal. Use rocks to prop the station in an upright position to prevent domestic animals from getting to the poison.

For a wood box bait station, you will need:

4 pine boards, ¾ inch x 5½ inches x 24 inches (1.9 cm x 14 cm x 61 cm), for the box sides, top, and bottom

2 pine boards, ¾ inch x 4 inches x 5 inches (1.9 cm x 10.2 cm x 14 cm), for the box ends

2 hinges, ¾ inch x 1 inch (1.9 cm x 2.5 cm)

1 hook and latch

1 box finishing nails

1 box 2½-inch (6.4-cm) drywall screws

Tools

hammer
drill and bits
screwdriver
3-inch (7.6-cm) hole cutter

1. Place one of the 5½x24-inch boards on a flat surface in front of you. Set a second 5½x24-inch board along the 24-inch side of the first board at a 90-degree angle. Nail the two boards together. Nail the third 5½x24-inch board to the other 24-inch side of the first board at a 90-degree angle. Nail the 4x5-inch boards over the ends to create an open box.
2. To form the top, use the hinges to secure the last 5½x24-inch board to one of the box sides. Attach the hinges with drywall screws.

3. On the edge of the box top opposite the hinges, install the hook. Add the latch closure to the box side, just below the hook.

4. Use a drill to cut a 3-inch (7.6-cm) diameter hole in the center of each end of the box.

5. Open the lid and set the poison or bait in the center. If you are using foot traps, place them close to the ends, near the 3-inch holes.

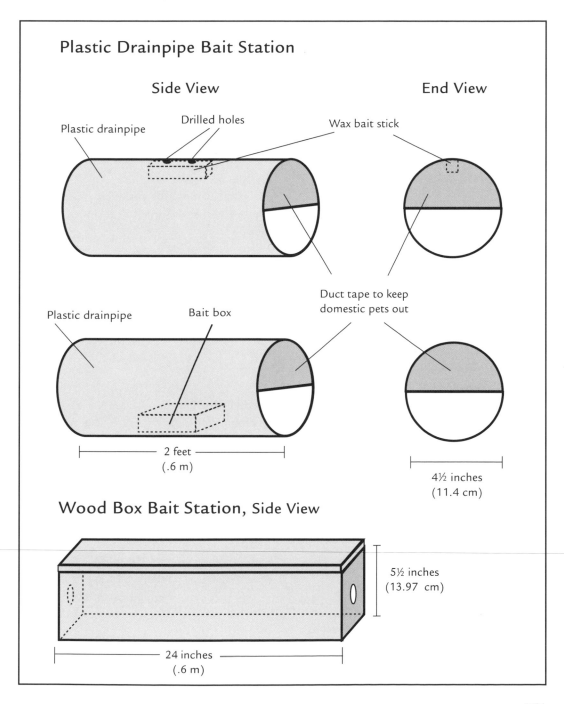

Plastic Drainpipe Bait Station

Side View   End View

Plastic drainpipe   Drilled holes   Wax bait stick

Duct tape to keep domestic pets out

Plastic drainpipe   Bait box

2 feet
(.6 m)

4½ inches
(11.4 cm)

Wood Box Bait Station, Side View

5½ inches
(13.97 cm)

24 inches
(.6 m)

Product Manufacturers

Body Gripping Traps
Conibear
Woodstream Corp.
Lititz, PA 17543
Phone: 717-626-2125

Gas Bombs
Giant Destroyer
Atlas Chemical Corp.
Box 141
Cedar Rapids, IA 52406
Phone: 319-377-8921

Glue Traps
Victor Glue Boards
Woodstream Corp.
Lititz, PA 17543
Phone: 717-626-2125

Rat and Mouse Tanglefoot Glue Boards
The Tanglefoot Co.
314 Straight Ave. SW
Grand Rapids, MI 49504
Phone: 616-459-4130

Leg Hold Traps
Victor, Oenida, Newhouse
Woodstream Corp.
Lititz, PA 17543
Phone: 717-626-2125

Live Traps
Havahart Traps
Woodstream Corp.
Lititz, PA 17543
Phone: 717-626-2125

Mole Traps
Victor Mole Trap
Woodstream Corp.
Lititz, PA 17543
Phone: 717-626-2125

Repellents
BioMet 12
M&T Chemical
PO Box 1194
Rahway, NJ 07065
Phone: 201-479-0200

Capsaicin
Hot Sauce Animal Repellent
Miller Chemical Corp.
Box 333
Hanover, PA 17331
Phone: 717-632-8921

Hinder
Leffingwell Co.
PO Box 1880
Brea, CA 92621

Methyl nonyl ketone
Market-Tech Industries
80 Skyline Dr.
Plainview, NY 11803
Phone: 516-433-2116

Paradichlorobenzene
Chacon Chemical Corp.
2600 Yates Ave.
City of Commerce, CA 90040
Phone: 213-721-5031

Polybutenes
Preferred Brand
Sun Pest Control
2945 McGee Trafficway
Kansas City, MO 64108
Phone: 816-561-2174

Putrescent whole egg solids
Deer Away
McLaughlin Gormley King Co.
712 15th Ave. NE
Minneapolis, MN 55413
Phone: 612-379-2895

ReJeX-iT
RJ Advantage
501 Murray Rd.
Cincinnati, OH 45217-1014
Phone: 1-800-423-3473

Tanglefoot
The Tanglefoot Co.
314 Straight Ave. SW
Grand Rapids, MI 49504
Phone: 616-459-4130

Tobacco Dust
Fasey & Besthoff Inc.
143 River Rd.
Edgewater, NJ 07020
Phone: 201-945-6200

Ziram
Rabbit Scat
Earl May Seed & Nursery Co.
208 N. Elm
Shenandoah, IA 516603
Phone: 712-246-1020

Scare Devices
Bird Bangers
Reed-Joseph International Co.
PO Box 894
Greenville, MS 38702
Phone: 1-800-647-5554

Bird Distress Calls
Johnny Stewart Wildlife Calls
5100 Fort Ave.
Waco, TX 76710
Phone: 254-772-3261

Electronic Guard
Pocatello Supply Depot
U.S. Fish and Wildlife Service
238 E. Dillon St.
Pocatello, ID 83201
Phone: 208-236-6920

Skunk Deodorants
Neutroleum Alpha
Pocatello Supply Depot
U.S. Fish and Wildlife Service
238 E. Dillon St.
Pocatello, ID 83201
Phone: 208-236-6920

Snap Traps
Victor
Woodstream Corp.
Lititz, PA 17543
Phone: 717-626-2125

Helpful Websites

www.wildlifecontrol.com
Wildlife Control of Long Island posts a pest control page, sells critter control supplies, and bird control products. This is a good place to go for information on bats, squirrels, geese, snakes, and raccoons.

www.deadduckdecoys.com
This is the place to get your geese decoys for goose control.

www.bugspray.com
Bug Spray posts articles on various pests and sells pest control supplies.

www.belllabs.com
Bell Laboratories is a good source for rodenticides, bait stations, glue boards, and plastic snap traps.

www.reedjoseph.com
Reed-Joseph International Company is a bird and wildlife control specialist and a great source for noisemakers, Bird Gard, and pyrotechnics such as bird bangers.

www.acenet.auburn.edu/department/ipm/ mammal.htm
The "Control of Mammals & Birds in the Vegetable Garden" provides information from the Alabama Cooperative Extension System. The site features a nice home and garden section.

www.deerbusters.com
Motion Activated Ultrasonic Devices is a major supplier of deer and animal control products, including repellents, fencing, scare devices, and ideas for mole and gopher control.

www.wctech.com
Wildlife Control Technology's home page and magazine is a great source for general critter control supplies.

www.oznet.ksu.edu
Wildlife Management Library of Kansas State University is a great management library, providing a wealth of downloadable information.

http://hammock.ifas.ufl.edu/txt/fair/16875
Wildlife Resources Handbook, operated by the University of Florida Cooperative Extension Service, provides great pest management guides.

www.havahart.com
Havahart home-page, posted by the manufacturer of live traps and other trapping supplies, provides good information on how to catch specific critters and sells many products.

www.fws.gov/idex.html
U.S. Fish and Wildlife Service operates this website and provides good information from a government viewpoint.

www.ippc.orst.edu/cicp/pests/rodents.htm
Database of IPM Resources–Rodents, posted by Oregon State University Integrated Plants Protection Center provides information on Pacific Northwest pest management.

http://ndsuext.nodak.edu/extnews/ askext/wildpest.htm
North Dakota State University Extension Service provides good information on lawn and garden pests, including rabbits, rodents, snakes, and bats.

www.uwex.edu/disted/infosrce/birds.htm
Raccoon, Deer, Skunks, & Birds, a page posted by the University of Wisconsin Extension Service, provides good information on the critters mentioned above.

www.dec.state.ny
New York State Department of Environmental Conservation's site provides a wealth of information, including wildlife protection laws.

www.ianr.unl.edu/pubs/wildlife/
Cooperative Extension Service–Institute of Agriculture & Natural Resources is a wildlife management page posted by Nebraska University. It includes information on wildlife damage control, habitat improvement, urban wildlife, and diseases.

Index